250-76

Columbia University

Contributions to Education

Teachers College Series

No. 395

AMS PRESS

NEW YORK

SCHOOL PROVISION FOR INDIVIDUAL DIFFERENCES

POLICIES AND DATA NECESSARY

BY

KNUTE O. BROADY, Ph.D.

144039

TEACHERS COLLEGE, COLUMBIA UNIVERSITY
CONTRIBUTIONS TO EDUCATION, No. 395

BUREAU OF PUBLICATIONS
Teachers College, Columbia University
NEW YORK CITY
1930

Library of Congress Cataloging in Publication Data

Broady, Knute Oscar, 1898-
   School provision for individual differences.

   Reprint of the 1930 ed., issued in series: Teachers
College, Columbia University. Contributions to
education, no. 395.
   Originally presented as the author's thesis, Columbia.
   Bibliography: p.
   1. Mentally handicapped children--Education--United
States. 2. Ability grouping in education.
3. Personnel service in education. I. Title.
II. Series: Columbia University. Teachers College.
Contributions to education, no. 395.
LC4691.B7 1972   371.9   71-176591

ISBN 0-404-55395-8

Reprinted by Special Arrangement with Teachers
College Press, New York, New York

From the edition of 1930, New York
First AMS edition published in 1972
Manufactured in the United States

AMS PRESS, INC.
NEW YORK, N. Y.   10003

ACKNOWLEDGMENTS

The writer is deeply indebted to the chairman of his dissertation committee, Professor Paul R. Mort, for his generous assistance and his constructive criticism. Professor Mort's work in the field of administrative provision for individual differences has been invaluable in this study.

The writer is likewise grateful to Professor N. L. Engelhardt for many evident and tangible expressions of confidence; to Professor George D. Strayer for his ever challenging stimulus; to Professors Harry D. Kitson and Ralph B. Spence for critical and searching analysis; and to Professors Carter Alexander and Willard S. Elsbree for constant interest and encouragement.

K. O. B.

CONTENTS

SCHOOL PROVISION FOR INDIVIDUAL DIFFERENCES

POLICIES AND DATA NECESSARY

CHAPTER I

THE PROBLEM AND THE METHOD OF ATTACK

People of almost every age and type are seeking admission to our public schools. Although educators are welcoming them they are at the same time actively proceeding to organize and differentiate the school organization so that the tens of millions who enroll will have available the educational facilities which their extremely diverse interests, abilities, and needs indicate to be desirable. Differentiation of instruction; the rapid development of vocational schools and junior and senior high schools; the provision of classes and schools for young workers, adults, the foreign-born, the mentally and physically handicapped, and the exceptionally able mentally are all tangible evidences of remarkable progress in this broadening of educational opportunity.

As our cities, towns, and rural areas differentiate their educational offerings in this manner so necessary to meet the needs of a tremendously heterogeneous school population, the problem of properly adjusting the school organization to each individual becomes most acute. In fact, the greater the differentiation of educational opportunities, the greater the danger of maladjustment. The normal child of ten years, for instance, is obviously better off in the most inflexible type of fifth grade or even third grade than he is if mistakenly placed with a group of mental subnormals. It would, theoretically, be possible for a school system to be equipped ideally according to the present point of view and to be furnishing, outwardly, striking evidence of the wealth of educational opportunity in the community, and yet for every child to be misplaced. Conditions are never so bad as that, but scores of school surveys and superintendents' reports have shown evidences of maladjustment, so serious as to demand immediate action. There is also the more constructive consideration, the challenge not only to guard against glaring maladjustment but to secure a degree of adaptation of school to pupil that was never possible with our less flexible and less varied types of organization.

Educators have formulated policies concerning the placement and progress of every type of individual seeking the benefits of the public school so that the educational facilities that have become rapidly available may be used to best advantage. Educators have sought to codify, provisionally, the traffic regulations, as it were, of American education. Experimental evidence, practical experience, and good judgment have been of great assistance in this task.

There will be continuous reformulation of these policies so long as new evidence becomes available and so long as education remains a growing and changing institution adapting itself in ever better fashion to our dynamic civilization. This prospect of rapid change in accepted educational procedure does not, however, destroy the value of a periodic statement of best theory and practice at any one time relative to adaptation of the schools to individual differences and needs. Such a formulation of present best opinion and practice is one of the contributions made by this study.

The policies collected and evaluated are those which specify in each instance first, a type of individual for whom adjustment should be made and, second, the specific adjustment needed. The necessity for adjustment may be due to one or more of a variety of causes. Mental or physical traits, chronological age, financial needs, and social abilities are only a few of those included. The types of adjustment demanded range all the way from exclusion to a specific adaptation to be made to the child within the classroom. Illustrative policies chosen at random from the various chapters show a few of the controlling factors and the recommended adjustments:

1. The hearing ability of suspected mental subnormals should be carefully determined before assignment to a special class is finally decided upon. (p. 15.)
2. The following children, whose physical condition warrants it, should attend summer elementary school classes:
   a. Those not already too much under-age who may secure a double promotion by attendance.
   b. Those who have been promoted but whose work is weak in certain subjects.

c. Those who are being given a trial promotion.

d. Those who will be given a trial promotion if they attend summer school. (p. 28.)

3. Specific training for the future occupation should increase in amount as the time for its use approaches, whereas general training should correspondingly decrease. (p. 50.)

4. Those who fall greatly below the class average should be assigned only the most essential of new material. (p. 60.)

Each of these policies, it is seen, recommends a specific adjustment to a specific type of individual. This was the criterion for the inclusion of the policies to be dealt with in this study. Policies pertaining to general administration and organization were excluded. The desirability of certain types of administration and organization may be discerned in some cases but that outcome is secondary.

Suggested policies were obtained first from educational literature. The 1926, 1927, and early 1928 files of the *Elementary School Journal, Journal of Educational Psychology, Journal of Educational Research, School Review* and *Teachers College Record* were consulted for representative magazine comment. Books, yearbooks, bulletins, and superintendents' annual reports known or thought to deal with the problem were searched, as were all available school surveys, and also more than one hundred unpublished dissertations and theses from universities having outstanding departments of education and psychology. All suggested policies of the type defined above found in this literature were recorded. These policies were arranged according to the kind of adjustment suggested. Contiguous with each policy was space for recording the reactions of people to be interviewed later.

The author then visited eighteen cities for the purpose of observation and conference. The superintendents, and those designated by them or their immediate assistants as most competent in each field of inquiry, were interviewed. Policies which the author had already formulated were carefully criticized by these people and other policies were suggested. Note was taken of policies in operation to the satisfaction of those concerned. The cities personally visited were Binghamton, Bronxville, Buffalo, Mount Vernon, New Rochelle, New York City (individual public and private schools), Rochester, and Scarsdale in the state of New York; Cleveland, Cleveland Heights, Lakewood, and Toledo in

Ohio; Montclair and Newark in New Jersey; Baltimore, Detroit, Philadelphia (individual schools) and Pittsburgh. Members of the faculty of Teachers College, Columbia University, gave freely of their time to the consideration of sections of the study in which they considered their assistance of most worth. Specialists outside the cities visited gave additional attention to the problem of kindergarten and first grade entrance and promotion, and to guidance. Several graduate students of Teachers College, Columbia University, who had held, or were at that time holding, positions of major responsibility in city systems were also interviewed.

The final tabulation of responses, made at the conclusion of the conferences, revealed first, the extent to which agreement existed in regard to the policies suggested in the literature that had been previously examined and second, the extent to which policies suggested in the field were assented to by those subsequently interviewed. A policy was deemed acceptable when those who endorsed it outnumbered those who opposed it. Except for details there was relatively little disagreement. This was probably to be expected, inasmuch as the policies, in general, were originally suggested by persons who ranked as authorities or were formulated as a result of careful experimentation.

The policies presented, it is thus seen, are based on such expert opinion and scientific evidence as the author was able to secure. These policies have an immediate value as guides to administrative procedure. Their usefulness will be enhanced if they are modified as other and more reliable evidence becomes available.

It is evident that the policies have another value in that they serve as the basis upon which to build a system of child accounting. Because most of the facts that are gathered about pupils are for the purpose of better adjusting the school to them, it is logical that suggested adjustments should be scrutinized in order to determine, first, the data necessary for the carrying out of these adjustments, second, when these data are to be recorded, and third, concerning whom these data should be obtained. The last chapter of this study includes the summary of such an analysis. An examination of the policies showed that pupil data must be gathered, and the particular adjustments made by the school staff determined. Pupil facts, checked against school adjustments which have been made, determine the extent to which the school is adapting itself to individual abilities and needs.

CHAPTER II

PROVISION FOR THOSE WHO ARE MENTALLY AND SCHOLASTICALLY SUBNORMAL

The policies stated in this and the seven following chapters were obtained by the methods of selection, evaluation, and reformulation described on the preceding pages. These methods are further explained and illustrated in the appendix. The most apparent and logical order of material determined the arrangement of policies by chapters.

POLICIES

I. PROVISION FOR THOSE WHO ARE MENTALLY SUBNORMAL

A. BASES FOR ADMISSION TO SPECIAL CLASSES

1. 1. The upper intelligence limit for entrance to a class for mental subnormals should be an I. Q. of 75 or 80. The lower limit should be an I. Q. of 50 or 55, with the provision that children showing a distinct foreign language handicap may enter with an I. Q. as low as 45.

2. a. The I. Q. obtained from a group test should be confirmed by at least one individual intelligence test, given by a competent examiner.

3. b. If teacher judgment does not confirm the test findings, the child should be kept in the regular class for further observation.

4. 2. Children below 45 or 50 I. Q. should be excluded from school and, if the parents consent, be placed in an institution for the feeble-minded.

5. a. Exclusion should take place only after several individual retests, followed by thorough observation, have convinced the school authorities that the child is uneducable.

5

6. 3. Remediable physical defects should be corrected before admitting the child to the special class, if there are any grounds for believing that these influences are unduly depressing the intelligence rating.

7. 4. After a child has been placed in a special class his intelligence rating should be frequently redetermined and he should be carefully observed for indications of ability to work with the lower normal group.

B. PROCEDURE WHEN A SPECIAL CLASS IS NOT POSSIBLE

8. 1. Numbers of subnormals in a given school system or attendance area may be too few to make feasible the organization of a special class. When such is the case teachers should provide for the subnormal child in the regular classroom, giving him individual attention when he cannot participate with the regular group and allowing him to progress at his own rate.

C. GRADING SPECIAL CLASS STUDENTS

9. 1. When more than one class for subnormals is maintained in a given building, the children should be graded either according to mental age or educational age. The mental or educational age range of each class will depend on the number to be sectioned and the size of class allowed.

10.   *a.* There should be a smaller number in classes for subnormals than in regular classes.

D. AGE OF ENTRANCE

11. 1. No child should be transferred to a class for subnormals until after he has attended the first grade for a year, unless his intelligence is so low as to unmistakably indicate him to be of calibre suited to subnormal classes.

12. 2. Unless transportation is provided, special class children below the tenth or eleventh year chronologically should attend schools near their homes.

13.   *a.* Children who are considerably under-size and are among the lowest mentally may be retained a year, or even two years, longer in the schools near their homes before being sent to schools at a distance.

E. Organizations to be provided

14. 1. Children from eleven to thirteen or fourteen years of age may be taken to elementary centers or placed in a section in the same school made up of older children. Provision should be made in junior high schools or pre-vocational schools for those above thirteen or fourteen.

15.   *a.* Boys and girls should, for educational and social reasons, be segregated after the age of thirteen or fourteen.

16.   *b.* If the number of subnormals is sufficient, pre-vocational schools should be provided. If there are too few to permit the establishment of such schools, special provision for pre-vocational work should be made in the regular junior high schools. Subnormals may be placed with normal groups in those activities in which they have sufficient ability to meet the competition they must thereby face.

17. 2. Approximately half the day should be spent in instruction in the tool subjects. It is to be expected that the level of attainment reached will be much lower than in regular schools.

18. 3. The remainder of the day should be spent in general manual or trade training, the type of work depending on the age of the child. The teaching of highly specialized vocations is not feasible, even in the later years.

19. 4. Such special abilities as the children reveal should be developed to a maximum degree in order to make the children useful members of society.

II. Coaching Groups in the Elementary School

A. How coaching should be provided

20. 1. Coaching may be carried on either by the regular class teacher or by a special coaching teacher. If a special coaching teacher is employed, she will generally work with the child at periods when he can best be spared from the regular classroom. Only rarely will she keep the child full-time. Pertinent data concerning the child who needs coaching should be secured by all agencies available to the school for such purposes.

21. 2. So far as possible, pupils should be given assistance before they fail.

22. 3. Pupils should be returned to the regular group when the deficiency has been corrected.

B. PUPILS FOR WHOM COACHING SHOULD BE PROVIDED

23. 1. Special coaching should be given the following groups:

24.   *a.* Those who, because of absence, entrance late in the term, or for other reasons, have fallen behind their classes.

25.   *b.* Those who have been promoted, but who have failed in important aspects of the work in the preceding grade.

26.   *c.* Those who have been given a special promotion, but have thereby skipped important aspects of work which must be made up.

27.   *d.* Those for whom special promotion is planned, provided they can cover sufficient work in advance.

28.   *e.* Those who are just able to work with their class and who must give more than the usual amount of time to mechanical skills.

29.   *f.* Those for whom enrichment has been deemed desirable.

30. 2. The following pupils should be put in full-time coaching classes. They will re-enter regular classes as soon as their deficiencies are corrected and they have sufficiently improved in their work to enable them to work readily with groups with whom they are not seriously maladjusted chronologically.

31.   *a.* Those who are, to a marked degree, socially and physically over-age when they enter school.

32.   *b.* Those who are very much retarded because of poor previous schooling.

III. COACHING GROUPS IN THE SECONDARY SCHOOL

33. 1. Pupils above subnormality who have fallen below or have failed to reach acceptable standards in the tool subjects may be brought together daily during a regular school period to acquire the skills that are considered necessary.

34.   *a.* If there are a sufficient number with a similar type of deficiency, a special class may be organized to remedy their particular difficulty.

35.   *b.* If deficiencies vary widely, as they usually do, children with various difficulties should enroll in the same class and individually acquire the skills which they lack.

36.   *c.* The school may organize a series of short courses, six, nine, or twelve weeks in length, to bring pupils up to grade in work in which they failed to obtain sufficient skill during the preceding semester. Thus, retardation for the sake of acquiring certain skills may be avoided.

37.   *d.* As soon as a satisfactory level of attainment is reached the student should be transferred from the coaching class to the regular class.

38. 2. Pupils, unable to master a subject in which they are already enrolled, may shift to a special diagnostic class during the remainder of the semester, there to remain under the close observation of the teacher. When the difficulty is removed the pupil should be transferred back to the regular class. Those whose difficulties cannot be removed should be required to drop the subject in which they are deficient and take up another.

39.   *a.* Other students who, in the judgment of the teachers, cannot master a subject as regularly taught may go into a special diagnostic class first, there to receive the help that will enable them to proceed with the regular class.

40. 3. Provided periods are long enough and teachers have sufficient skill, part or all of this corrective work may be done in conjunction with the teaching of certain courses. The English teacher, for example, may bring pupils up to grade in English, spelling, writing, and reading.

IV. Special Purpose Classes in the Secondary School
for Low-Ability Students

41. 1. Special curricular opportunities should be provided pupils who are just above subnormality. These pupils will often enter

junior high school a year or more over-age and will usually have the ability of a normal fourth- or fifth-grade child.

42.   *a.* Children just above subnormality can be grouped most readily when the number of ability groups is so large that the lowest section contains only pupils of that type.

43.   *b.* In such classes no thought should be given to college entrance work. Attention should be devoted solely to activities that will in and of themselves be most useful.

44.   *c.* When neither the low-ability nor the normal pupils suffer thereby, the work should be given with the regular class group.

45.   2. There is much to be said in favor of only partial departmentalization for low-ability pupils during their first year or two of junior high school. The pupils may stay with one teacher for their academic work and go to different instructors for other activities.

CHAPTER III

EDUCATION FOR THE PHYSICALLY HANDICAPPED

1. 1. Certain children, who are physically handicapped, such as epileptics, or the totally blind or deaf, have no place in the regular school organizations.

2. 2. Inasmuch as the physically handicapped whose education is a function of the school may generally look forward to becoming wholly or partially self-supporting, their education should have as definite and valid a vocational outlook for them as the regular educational program has for the normal group. Their education should also enable them to look forward to as real and full an enjoyment of life as does the normal group.

3. 3. When there are too few pupils with a particular handicap to make advisable the organization of a special class, the regular class teacher should approximate in the regular classroom the adaptations that are usually made in the special rooms.

4.   *a.* The most severe cases may occasionally be educated in their homes, with the help of a visiting teacher. Groups that may be considered for such services are:

5.   (1) Cardiacs—either partial bed cases or permanent.

6.   (2) Cripples who, because of special deformities, are unable to leave their homes.

7.   (3) Discharged hospital patients requiring home coaching during convalescence to help them to remain at their grade level.

8.   (4) Cardiacs or cripples who, because of their early physical condition, have never attended school and who are now sufficiently improved physically soon to be able to go to school.

I. Cripples

A. Facilities to be provided

9. 1. Cities under 50,000 must usually care for their cripples in regular classrooms or send them to special institutions or in rare instances, send a visiting teacher to their homes for individual instruction; cities from 50,000 to 300,000 or thereabouts may establish special classes, while the largest cities may, with an adequate system of transportation, have special schools.

10. 2. Transportation to and from school is necessary, as is provision for the special needs of the cripples within the building.

11. 3. Crippled children who are so badly handicapped as to require hospital care may be taught at public expense in hospital classes.

12. 4. Corrective rooms may well be provided for cripples in junior and senior high school.

13. 5. Crippled children who are preparing for vocations should be trained in work suited as nearly as possible to their ability to perform, as well as to their interests and aptitudes.

B. Types for whom provision should be made

14. 1. There should be special school provision for permanently crippled children who are unable to attend regular school because of inability to get there and who require special facilities for seating and working when they are transported.

15.   a. No child who is suffering from a disease in its active stages, such as acute and tender poliomyelitis or acute tubercular orthopedic lesions, should attend a public school.

II. Partially-Sighted

A. Facilities to be provided

16. 1. Limitations, attributable to school enrollment, in regard to the organization of special classes and schools for partially-sighted children are much the same as for cripples.

17.   a. Where the number enrolled warrant, grading may be carried out on the basis of mental age, with due refer-

ence to previous school training, type of physical defect, and other qualifying factors.

18. 2. Furniture, class schedule, instructional materials, blackboard writing, course of study, and illumination of the classroom, all must be adapted to the peculiar needs of partially-sighted children.

19. 3. Partially-sighted children may advantageously remain full time in their special classes.

20. 4. Rate of academic progress may be somewhat less for the partially-sighted pupils than for normal pupils.

21. 5. So far as possible, vocational preparatory courses best adapted to their needs should be offered during the secondary school years.

B. TYPES FOR WHOM PROVISION SHOULD BE MADE

22. 1. By general definition those who should be in sight-saving classes are:

23. *a.* Those whose vision will not permit the use of ordinary school equipment, assuming an attempt to correct vision with glasses.

24. *b.* Those whose vision would suffer serious impairment should they be compelled to use ordinary school equipment, even with attempted correction by means of glasses.

25. 2. The most recent specific standards advise the entrance of:

26. *a.* Children who cannot read more than 20/70 on a standard Snellen chart in the better eye, or who cannot read No. 2.00 at 20 cm.

27. *b.* Myopes who have more than 6 diopters at ten years of age or under.

28. *c.* Children who have 3 diopters of myopia which is progressive.

29. *d.* Hyperopes who have symptoms of asthenopia and whose vision in the better eye falls below 20/70.

30.   *e.* Children who have an astigmatism of more than 3.5 diopters and whose vision cannot be brought up to more than 20/70 in the better eye.

31.   *f.* Children with corneal opacities whose vision is 20/50 or less in the better eye.

32.   *g.* Cases of inactive keratitis where vision is 20/50 or less in the better eye.

33.   *h.* Children having congenital cataracts, secondary cataracts, congenital malformation, or fundus lesions where no acute condition is present, with vision of 20/50 or less in the better eye.

34.   *i.* Any child who, in the oculist's opinion, would benefit by sight-saving training should be accepted for treatment or training, subject to the suggestions of the oculist.

Note:

35.   (1) It is assumed that these conditions exist after the proper refractions have been made.

36.   (2) One good eye constitutes non-eligibility for sight-saving classes.

37. 3. As soon as children have been brought above levels set as admission standards to the special classes, they should be put into the regular classroom unless, in the opinion of the specialists, the work in sight conservation promises better opportunity for conserving remaining vision.

38. 4. As a means of supplementing the work of medical examiners, teachers and nurses should be on the alert to detect and refer to the examiner such indications of eyestrain as headaches, blepharitis, eye fatigue, nervous symptoms, frowning or squinting, and lachrymation.

39. 5. Children suffering from trachoma should be isolated.

40. 6. Eyesight of children suspected of low mentality should be tested.

41. 7. Quite generally the mental subnormals who are also visually defective must be kept in the classes for the visual defec-

tives because there are too few who are subnormal, both mentally and visually, to make satisfactory segregation possible.

42. 8. Children who are totally blind or who have a visual acuity of 1/10 or less should be placed in a special class or institution for the blind where provision is made for education and vocations suited to the blind.

III. Deafened Children

43. 1. Approximately ten per cent of the children attending school are noticeably handicapped by deafness.

44. 2. The hearing ability of those suspected of mental subnormality should be carefully determined before assignment to a special class is finally decided upon.

45. 3. As a means of supplementing the regular otological examinations, the teachers and school nurse should look for such symptoms of hearing difficulty as cotton in the child's ear or his sitting in such a position as to favor his hearing.

A. Types for Whom Provision Should Be Made

46. 1. In general there are five groups for whom special provision should be made. They are:

47.   *a.* Congenitally deaf children who should be in special schools for the deaf.

48.   (1) Others of the deafened group for whom a special institution may be necessary are:

49.   (*a*) Those whose home conditions are unsuitable for their rearing;

50.   (*b*) Those who are incorrigible or mentally deficient;

51.   (*c*) Those who do not live in the vicinity of a day school;

52.   (*d*) Those incapable of learning speech.

53.   *b.* Children with less than twenty-five per cent of normal hearing ability who can hear only when the voice is spoken directly into the ear. Such children require lip reading and grade instruction in small special classes.

54.   *c.* Children who are hard of hearing but who hear raised voices at close range (about five feet). They should spend a period each day in mastering lip reading and will also require coaching in their school work.

55.   *d.* Children who are slightly deaf who hear conversational tones at about six feet. They should also spend a period a day in mastering lip reading.

56.   *e.* Children who are intermittently deaf and whose primary need is medical treatment. Medical aid should be extended whenever it will be of any value.

57.   2. Children belonging to groups (*c*) and (*d*) above should under no consideration be placed in special full-time schools for the deafened. They would, by that arrangement, lose the very contact which they most need, the contact with normal children.

58.   3. When the 4-A Audiometer is used in determining auditory acuity, a hearing loss of six sensation units may be considered suspicious if there is any history of family deafness, while a loss of nine sensation units may be regarded as indicating a potential case of deafness. A loss of more than nine sensation units indicates definitely impaired hearing.

59.   4. Lip reading should be given when the otological examination shows a possible progressive or a chronic catarrhal condition or gives indication of even slight nerve deafness.

60.   5. Some of those who have even a very low degree of auditory acuity may, if they acquire a high degree of facility in lip reading, be given a trial in the regular grade classes.

61.   6. If those among the deafened who go beyond elementary school have mastered the technique of lip reading by the time they are ready for advanced education, they may take work very similar to that pursued by normal children.

62.   *a.* If they have not mastered lip reading by the time they reach high school or college they should do so at the earliest opportunity.

63.   7. A few general principles that deafened pupils may well follow in the selection of a vocation are:

64.   *a.* Music, and the arts most closely associated with it, such as the drama, should generally be shunned.

65.   *b.* Occupations in which hearing is the important factor should be avoided. Among these are work with the telephone, telegraph, or radio, and dictograph operating and stenography.

66.   *c.* Factors that must be considered, aside from the job itself, are type and degree of the pupil's deafness, the possibilities for the conservation of his remaining hearing power, his attitude toward his own deafness, and the question of continuance in the occupation with steadily diminishing hearing.

67. 8. Since there is the possibility of eyestrain due to lip reading, careful watch over eyesight should be maintained by the classroom teachers. Children so affected should be seated near the front of the room when in their regular classes.

IV. Fresh Air Classes

A. Facilities to be provided

68. 1. Both open-air and open-window classes may be used as means of rehabilitating certain groups of students.

69. 2. Sleep and wholesome food contribute quite largely to the recuperation of those who attend fresh air classes.

70. 3. The physical defects of those enrolled in the fresh air classes should, so far as possible, be removed.

71. 4. There are usually enough children needing the advantages of fresh air classes to make feasible the organization of a fresh air class for each large elementary school and for each two or three small elementary schools.

72. 5. Physical condition, as well as mental and educational age, may be used as a basis for sectioning when such is possible.

73. 6. Nutrition and fresh air classes will generally not be provided in high school. Children should, by the time they arrive at high school age, have passed and overcome a good deal of the illness and frailty that makes fresh air classes necessary in the grades.

B. WHO SHOULD ATTEND FRESH AIR CLASSES

74. 1. Those who actually have pulmonary tuberculosis must be isolated in fresh air classes throughout their school careers.

75. 2. Others who may well be in fresh air classes are:

76.   *a.* Those exposed to an open case of tuberculosis at present or recently.

77.   *b.* Those with closed tuberculosis in any organ, without known exposure.

78.   *c.* Those who have had tuberculosis, now arrested or cured.

79.   *d.* Children who are thin, frail, anemic, nervous, always tired, or susceptible to colds at frequent intervals.

80.   *e.* Children who are suffering from malnutrition.

81.   *f.* Children who are convalescing, especially from respiratory tract diseases.

82.   *g.* Children suffering from cardiac diseases.

83.   *h.* Children suffering from nervous diseases.

84. 3. All children who are ten per cent or more underweight may be considered for entrance to fresh air classes.

85.   *a.* If no improvement in weight results, the child should be referred to the school physician for further examination and treatment, if such is necessary.

86.   *b.* As children improve in weight they should be considered for reinstatement in their regular class groups.

87. 4. Children who are orthopedic cases of the inactive type and are able to move about quite freely may attend fresh air classes if classes for cripples cannot be organized. This is particularly true of those who have tubercular bone lesions.

88. 5. Removal of the deficiencies that bring children into the fresh air classes should usually be the basis for their return to the normal group.

89. 6. Classification of children in fresh air classes should be made on the basis of mental ability or achievement, with due reference to physical condition.

V. Cardiac Cases

A. Facilities to be provided

90. 1. Cardiacs may be in fresh air classes with under-nourished and pre-tubercular children or they may be in classes by themselves where they will have a daily regimen suited to their physical capacities.

91. *a.* The types of exercise calculated to best strengthen the heart should also be given.

92. 2. There may be classes in the hospitals for children who are too seriously ill to attend school or for those who live over such widely scattered areas that the organization of special classes near the home is not possible.

93. 3. When there are too few students for a special class, regular classroom teachers must make such provision for them as they can in the regular classroom.

B. Groups for whom provision should be made

94. 1. Admission may be granted to:

95. *a.* All congenital cases.

96. *b.* Potential cases.

97. (1) With history of acute rheumatism.

98. (2) With two of the following symptoms present: tonsilitis, myositis, growing pains or joint pains.

99. (3) With severe recurring choreas.

100. (4) With heart murmurs and definite valvular lesions.

VI. Speech Difficulties

A. Facilities to be provided

101. 1. The regular classroom teacher can eradicate most of the speech defects found among children just entering school.

102. 2. Special classes, meeting several times a week, will serve to eliminate the more severe and tenacious defects in speaking.

103. 3. Those who are most severely afflicted should be enrolled

in full-time special classes or in special schools, if numbers make that possible.

104. *a.* The number may be sufficient to permit grading according to achievement and intelligence as well as according to types of special defects.

B. Types for whom provision should be made

105. 1. Classes meeting several times weekly for speech correction exercises should be composed of those whose defects are not so serious as to cause embarrassment and inhibition of normal activity in the presence of normal children.

106. 2. Those who have acute cases of lalling, stammering, and similar defects, and who would suffer further difficulty in speech and increasing nervousness by remaining in regular classes, should be in full-time special classes.

107. 3. Speech defects for which correction should be sought in one manner or another may be classified as follows:

108.   *a.* The nervous speech disorders, under which come stammering, stuttering, cluttering, and nervous hesitation.

109.   *b.* Retarded speech in both normal and subnormal children.

110.   *c.* Infantile substitutions not caused by mouth malformation.

111.   *d.* Substitution of sounds or imperfect speech caused by malformations of the speech organs.

112.   *e.* Voice defects, not organic.

113.   *f.* Voice defects after certain operations, such as cleft palate or adenoids.

114.   *g.* Imperfect speech, through partial deafness.

115.   *h.* Aphasia, sensory or motor.

116.   *i.* Foreign substitution of speech sounds, caused by foreign environment.

117.   *j.* Sluggish enunciation attributable to poor muscular coördination, which may possibly have been caused by certain diseases of childhood.

VII. LEFT-HANDED PUPILS

118. Lighting and seating should be so arranged for left-handed children that they may write with the advantages given to right-handed children and in a position corresponding to that maintained by right-handed children.

VIII. EPILEPTICS

119. Children who have had epileptic attacks within the preceding six months should not be admitted even to special classes. Such instruction as these children secure should be given by the visiting teacher in the home or in small hospital classes.

IX. BEHAVIOR AND TRUANCY PROBLEMS

120. 1. A thorough physical, medical, psychological, and psychiatrical study of the delinquent, followed by a satisfactory curriculum, will do much to bring about adjustment of the child to the school.

121. *a.* Moving the child to another school and hence another environment may be effective.

122. 2. The following pupils may be considered to fall in groups needing these adjustments:

123. *a.* Those who consistently fail in their studies.

124. *b.* Disciplinary cases.

125. *c.* Chronic truants.

126. *d.* Social inadequates.

127. 3. In extreme cases, especially where the home environment is absolutely nonconducive to reform, the provision of completely new surroundings may be necessary. Parental or truant schools may be the logical necessity.

X. PSYCHOPATHIC CASES

128. 1. If the difficulty is extremely serious, it may be advisable for the child to be taken from home for a time at least.

129. 2. The disposition of children who show psychopathic difficulties had best be settled by a conference of specialists.

130.   3. The following cases, if serious in proportion, may call for psychopathic diagnoses:

131.   *a.* Temper tantrums.

132.   *b.* Stealing and lying.

133.   *c.* Sex problems.

134.   *d.* Suspected epileptics and chorea cases.

135.   *e.* Stuttering and stammering in special cases.

136.   *f.* Chronic truancy.

137.   *g.* Dementia præcox.

138.   *h.* Over-protection in the home.

CHAPTER IV

PROVISION FOR OTHER SPECIAL GROUPS

I. Vocational Education

A. Types of provision to be made

1. 1. In general, vocational and non-vocational students should be in separate classes.

2. 2. Vocational and non-vocational work may be carried forward simultaneously in some courses, such as the following:

3.   a. Those that prepare for homemaking.

4.   b. Those that prepare for business.

5.   c. Those that prepare for agriculture.

6.   d. Full-time trade curricula which extend over two or more years.

7.   e. Part-time coöperative curricula which extend over two or more years.

In such cases the vocational courses may be in the regular high schools.

8. 3. Among others, the following vocational courses should be given:

9.   a. Homemaking, which is common to all communities.

10.   b. Business occupations, which engage people almost everywhere.

11.   c. Agriculture in the rural areas.

12.   d. Shop courses, where the demand is sufficient.

13.   e. Training needed for employment in the manufacturing centers.

14. 4. In general, in determining vocational courses, the needs of the immediate, and the not so immediate, community should be considered.

15.   *a.* Where the population is a rapidly shifting one, the occupations represented in the vocational program should be those found over wide areas and in many communities.

16.   *b.* Where the shift of population and the turn-over of workers are not too great, it should be possible to recognize the dominant occupations of the community.

17.   *c.* Only in cities of considerable size or in those where the industry is highly specialized are there a sufficient number of boys who wish to prepare for some one of the trades to justify the expense of maintaining the necessary equipment and employing properly trained teachers. Vocational training should be of three types: (a) That which is intended to give the skills needed; (b) that which provides the related knowledge necessary for most intelligent application of the skills; (c) the social and economic knowledge peculiar to an occupational group.

B. Policies relative to vocational guidance

18. 1. The minimum age of entrance to vocational work should, whenever possible, be fixed at such a point as to permit pupils to finish by the end of the compulsory age limit.

19. 2. Entrance to vocational work should generally come at such a time that the pupils will finish the course just at the time they plan to leave school. In other words, vocational education should immediately precede employment at the occupation.

20. 3. Standards as to minimum intelligence, health, physical qualifications, general education, prerequisite skills and other qualifications should be set up for each of the vocations as rapidly as valid data may be secured.

21.   *a.* Boys and girls of the dull normal type or still lower in intelligence should generally not be considered for specialized vocational work. Such people should usually be given training in the general skills that will enable them to adapt themselves quickly to the numerous types of unskilled and semi-skilled positions they will fill.

22. *b.* Interests of the pupils should receive consideration in guidance.

23. 4. Attendance at continuation school will generally be compulsory, designed to serve boys and girls who are leaving the full-time school, but who are required by law to attend classes a certain number of hours each week.

24. *a.* The training received should usually supplement the training received in industry.

25. *b.* When the pupil is evidently a misfit in the work in which he is engaged, he should be trained for what he can do best.

26. *c.* As school record systems are made more complete, and adequate data concerning the child become more readily obtainable from the full-time school, a better determination may be made of what the continuation school training should be.

27. 5. Only those may enroll as indentured apprentices who have been accepted by an employer on that basis and thus have permission to attend school on his time. Indentured apprentices will take work in school that is directly related to their vocation.

28. 6. Pupils whom school and employers have agreed should be so educated and who have suitable qualifications for a given vocation attend on the coöperative basis.

II. Placement

29. 1. Children who quit school to enter remunerative employment should be guided into the occupations for which the school has sought to prepare them.

30. 2. Young people under eighteen years of age must often, for a time at least, enter an occupation not in line with their previous preparation. They should as quickly as possible transfer into their chosen occupations. Past preparation and future expectations should always be related to present employment.

31. 3. Guidance of the young worker should be continued after he has left school, perhaps until he is twenty-one years of age.

III. AFTERNOON AND EVENING CLASSES

32. 1. Afternoon and evening classes for adults should be organized in any subject in which interest is shown by a group large enough to form a class.

33. 2. Native or foreign-born illiterates who are beyond compulsory school age should be urged to attend classes both to avail themselves of general educational opportunities and to acquire facility in the use of English.

34. 3. Non-English speaking but literate foreigners should acquire skill in the use of English by attending afternoon or evening classes, thus to meet occupational or citizenship requirements.

35. *a.* They should be encouraged to continue their education beyond the mere acquisition of ability to read, write and speak English.

36. *b.* Mothers who have few contacts with those who speak English should be especially urged to attend. Special afternoon classes should be organized for them, if necessary.

37. *c.* Parents who are anxious to maintain an educational standing comparable to that of their children should be encouraged to attend afternoon or evening schools.

38. 4. If demand warrants it, factory classes should be held for workers immediately after working hours.

39. 5. Adults who are hard of hearing should be encouraged to attend classes in lip reading and those who have speech defects should be urged to seek the correction of these defects. Other physical handicaps should be overcome, so far as possible.

40. 6. If adults anticipate leaving their present work, they should have the opportunity to receive evening training in vocational work either along the line of their present vocation or for other vocations.

41. 7. Those who wish to complete their high school training, either in anticipation of college entrance or to qualify for a vocation, should be enrolled in accredited evening schools of secondary level.

42. 8. Young people who withdraw from school before completing their secondary work should be urged to continue in evening school. In no case, though, may evening school attendance be substituted for compulsory day school attendance.

43. 9. Grading and grouping in afternoon and evening schools should be carried out in much the same way as in day schools. The plan of grouping according to the purpose for which the course is taken may be used to good advantage. People of foreign birth who are receiving instruction to secure facility in the use of English should be grouped largely according to their ability in the use of that language.

IV. Classes for Non-English Speaking Children of School Age

44. 1. If the number of non-English speaking children is sufficient, they should be put in full-time special classes until they have attained sufficient command of the English language to enable them to make normal progress in the regular class groups.

45.   *a.* Provided there are enough of these children for several classes in one building, either ability in the use of the English language or educational or mental age, if they are determinable, may be used as bases for sectioning.

46.   *b.* Children passing out of these classes should, so far as possible, be with others of their own chronological age.

47.   (1) Exceptions will necessarily be made for those whose educational age is considerably below normal. These retarded pupils should, however, be brought into groups as near their chronological age as possible.

48. 2. If the number of non-English speaking children is not sufficient to permit the organization of a special class, coaching in the use of the English language should be supplied several times a week. In the meantime, children should be placed with others of approximately their own chronological age.

V. Summer Schools

49. 1. The following children, whose physical condition warrants it, should attend summer elementary school classes:

50.   *a.* Those not already too much under-age who may secure a double promotion by attendance.

51.   *b.* Those who have been promoted, but whose work is weak in certain subjects.

52.   *c.* Those who are being given a trial promotion.

53.   *d.* Those who will be given a trial promotion if they attend summer school.

54. 2. The school authorities must satisfy themselves that the child is not so low in his work that repetition the next year would be preferable to summer schooling with promotion following that.

55. 3. The following high school students, whose physical condition warrants it, should be encouraged to attend summer secondary school:

56.   *a.* Those who have failed in certain courses and are seeking to make up a deficiency in credits.

57.   *b.* Those who are not seriously under-age whose previous standing is satisfactory, and who wish to make additional credits.

58. 4. Specialized schools, such as commercial and continuation schools, may operate throughout the year with the regularly enrolled student group continuing through the summer months.

CHAPTER V

INSTRUCTIONAL ORGANIZATIONS AS MEANS OF PROVIDING FOR INDIVIDUAL DIFFERENCES

I. Ability Grouping

A. Extent of ability grouping

1. 1. Such evidence as has been assembled somewhat favors ability grouping, especially if content and method are adapted to the different ability levels.

2. 2. No minimum number of groups are necessary to make sectioning feasible, although three are more effective than two.

3. 3. Sectioning may take place early in the first grade if the children have attended kindergarten, or come later during that year if they have had no experience in kindergarten.

4. *a.* If both morning and afternoon kindergarten sessions are provided, those who are more mature socially, physically, and mentally may attend one of the sessions and the less mature, the other session. Thus a degree of homogeneity will be secured.

5. 4. Ability grouping should extend through the elementary school in so far as numbers within the grade make that possible.

6. 5. Ability grouping should be continued through the secondary school to the extent that the number taking a given subject make that possible and to the extent that such a procedure does not prevent making available an adequate variety of courses. Generally, increasing diversification will make ability grouping more difficult and less necessary as the upper years of high school are reached.

7. *a.* Bases for grouping should be modified according to the needs of each particular class.

8. 6. Grouping should be so conceived and so executed that stigmatization of those in the lower-ability groups is avoided.

9. 7. There is little evidence to substantiate the belief that grouping should be avoided in certain subjects or in certain activities in high school, provided sectioning is based on the proper criteria.

10. 8. Evidence and opinion are as yet more inconclusive in regard to the advisability of segregating children of exceptional intelligence than in regard to homogeneous grouping in general.

11.   *a.* The grouping of children high in other than abstract abilities has been advanced for consideration.

12. 9. Sectioning within a room according to ability in a particular activity is desirable, provided the groups organized are not so numerous as to interfere with the teacher's effective supervision of all students.

B. BASES FOR GROUPING IN THE ELEMENTARY SCHOOL

13. 1. Grouping should be based on objective measures of ability to perform, using E. Q., I. Q. or E. A., plus subjective measures of ability to perform, usually the teachers' judgments.

14.   *a.* The E. Q. if obtained from a battery of achievement tests, is practically as valid a measure of ability as the I. Q. obtained from a group test.

15.   *b.* If teacher judgment shows the child better able to perform than the objective measure indicates, the former should be given consideration. In fact, the child may well be placed in a section on the basis of the highest estimate of his ability, unless the reliability and validity of that estimate are open to serious question.

16.   *c.* Teacher's judgment may be made up of a composite ranking, including grades earned and estimates based on other observations, or it may be made up of two separate rankings, using grades for one and estimates based on other observations for the second.

17. 2. Factors such as pupil's interests, industry, physiological age, or health may be considered in sectioning by using the rule that if one falls greatly above or below the others, it should be given consideration. It is evident that these factors usually influence the teachers' estimate even though she is not aware of the fact. They should be given more conscious consideration.

18.   3. It is quite likely that, for sectioning within a class taught by one teacher, educational age is superior to either E. Q. or I. Q. In sectioning for the teaching of a single subject the E. A. obtained for that subject is probably the best basis.

19.   4. Chronological age alone is sometimes used as a basis for sectioning in kindergarten.

20.   5. A minimum I. Q. of 120 to 130 is usually considered essential for entrance to a class for gifted children.

21.   *a.* Poor physical condition, especially if aggravated by keenness of competition or distance of travel, should probably lead to the exclusion of some people otherwise well fitted for the work.

22.   *b.* Opinion as to the advisability of excluding children not outstanding in school achievement, but otherwise qualified for entrance to gifted classes, is not united. Each case must be settled on its own merits. If the child will meet the challenge of the special class and if it will spur him to his greatest effort, he should probably go into the special class.

23.   6. If the small school is to achieve ability grouping to any degree it must often section within the rooms for instructional purposes.

24.   7. If a pre-determined range of ability is used in defining each section, differentiation of the curriculum may be determined beforehand with a degree of accuracy. If, on the other hand, the range of ability within a certain section depends on the size of the whole class and, consequently, on the number of groups that may be formed from it, differentiation must be largely in the hands of the teacher.

25.   8. Over-ageness compensates to a certain extent for lack of ability; under-ageness is probably compensated for to the same degree by unusual ability. The consideration that Detroit suggests may be given chronological age in elementary and junior high school classification should be considered for adoption by other school systems.

C. BASES FOR GROUPING IN SECONDARY SCHOOL

26. 1. General ability grouping in secondary schools is based on the same criteria as are used in the elementary school. The basic data are objective measures of ability to achieve as determined by E. Q., I. Q., and E. A., plus subjective measures of the same ability as determined by previous grades and the teachers' estimates.

27. *a.* Less reliance may be placed on teachers' estimates when children enter from elementary schools which maintain widely diverse standards or enroll their pupils from social groups differing widely from school to school.

28. *b.* Chronological age affects grouping in the secondary school in the same way as in the elementary school, the younger pupils tending to be placed in lower ability groups and older pupils of the same mentality in the higher groups.

29. 2. Other factors, such as health rating, weight age, height age, dentition age, and social age are given consideration, provided they are obtainable and, if obtainable, provided their deviation from the basic factors is great.

30. 3. Attitude should be considered in grouping to the extent that a pupil who is a tireless worker with a high degree of tenacity, determination and interest can compensate to a certain extent for lack of a keen intellect. These factors quite naturally influence to some extent both teachers' grades and objective rating.

31. 4. If reading and language usage scores earned by the secondary school pupil fall significantly below the level reached by other criteria such facts may lead to placing the pupil in a lower ability group.

32. 5. The most recent valid and reliable measures of ability to perform should be used as bases for sectioning.

33. *a.* Grades earned in high school should, as they become available, be substituted for grade school record.

34. *b.* Grades earned in the more elementary subject matter levels are probably more significant criteria of future success than any other single basis for judgment.

35. 6. The purpose for which the pupils are taking a course should be considered in sectioning and, where the purpose is highly selective, may of itself be used as a basis for sectioning.

36. *a.* Pupils engaged in commercial work, technical education, preparation for a particular type of college entrance and agriculture, have a community of interests sufficient to create a degree of homogeneity both in interests and in ability.

37. *b.* So far as is feasible, ability grouping as determined by objective and subjective measures should be provided for within each purpose group.

38. 7. Outstanding specific ability in æsthetic intelligence, mechanical ability, leadership, social traits and creative writing, should serve as bases for grouping into classes to further develop the abilities enumerated.

39. *a.* The Seashore tests may be used in grouping for the development of musical ability.

40. *b.* Success in a verbal intelligence test has been reported to have considerable value in predicting ability in creative writing.

41. 8. Measures of ability to succeed in a given subject should be used as bases for grouping in that subject.

42. *a.* Prognostic tests have been developed, the scores from which have some value in predicting success in a given subject. Achievement tests based on a particular subject have prognostic value for more advanced phases of that subject.

43. *b.* Previous grades earned in a particular subject have considerable value for grouping in that subject.

D. BASES FOR GROUPING IN PHYSICAL EDUCATION

44. 1. Interclass teams should be matched either according to a Strength Index or exponent determined for each participant, or

according to "stunt" scores made by each pupil in qualifying for each game or, at least, each type of activity.

45.   *a.* Proper matching may be brought about either through equalizing the total scores or, preferably, by matching the indices or exponents of individuals on the competing teams.

46.   *b.* Upper and lower limits, as determined by the index of strength, should be set for each team.

47.   2. Physical fitness may be determined according to the formula:

$$\text{Physical Fitness} = \frac{\text{Individual Strength Index}}{\substack{\text{Normal Strength Index} \\ \text{for Age and Weight}}}$$

48.   3. With the measure determined for each pupil, the following policies should probably prevail:

49.   *a.* Boys in the ninth grade whose P. F. I.'s are above 120 should be excused from attendance at regular classes and possibly be given special training for leadership and made to function as class leaders.

50.   *b.* Boys in the seventh, eighth and ninth grades whose P. F. I.'s fall below 85 should be grouped and given an individual regimen and special attention from the physical director.

51.   *c.* The remaining groups in junior high school should be sectioned according to grade in school and further subdivided by means of the Strength Index for games and other group activity.

52.   *d.* In the senior high school, pupils with P. F. I.'s below 85 should receive the same general consideration as in junior high school.

53.   *e.* All boys in the senior high school with P. F. I.'s above 115 should be excused from regular class work, provided their disciplinary records merit it.

54.   *f.* Boys in the senior high school with P. F. I.'s of 85 to 99 should be required to spend three afternoon hour-

periods a week in physical education on days of their own choice, while those with P. F. I.'s of 100 to 114 should spend two afternoon hour-periods a week on days, and in activities, of their own choice.

55. 4. Boys should be chosen for interscholastic athletics according to an Index Score based on Strength Index, Physical Fitness Index, and Intelligence Quotient.

56. 5. Bases for homogeneous grouping of girls for physical education should, until evidence points to the contrary, depend on the same general criteria as for the boys.

II. The Use of Other Organizations in Adapting the School to Individual Differences

57. 1. Departmentalization may make possible the employment of teachers more skilled in particular phases of education. If means are at the same time provided for adequate gathering, pooling and making available to all the teaching staff significant individual pupil data, the school may thereby more adequately serve each boy and girl.

58. 2. Subject promotion establishes a degree of flexibility in the curriculum that enables the school to better select the activities in which each pupil should engage. Subject promotion should certainly begin in the junior high school.

59. *a.* Subject promotion will make it easier for a pupil to take work in the grade above or below the grade in which he is regularly enrolled.

60. 3. Under the plan of individual instruction some of the adjustments that may be made to different ability levels are:

61. *a.* Differentiated assignments.

62. *b.* More freedom for the abler pupils in the planning of their daily schedules, especially under the Dalton plan.

CHAPTER VI

ENTRANCE AND PROMOTION POLICIES

I. Promotion

1. 1. Children should be with those of approximately their own chronological age, except as other conditions dictate.

2. 2. National norms should receive little consideration in grading and promotion, except where children in the upper grades are involved and the question of college or further training is considered.

3. 3. Failure and repetition as a policy are not acceptable. All children should progress through their educational experiences at a rate suited to their abilities and none should find it necessary to repeat any extensive stage of their educational journey. Such a policy leads to one of two procedures for the dull pupils:

4.   *a.* They will spend more than six years in accomplishing six years work but the retardation will come about by the addition of semesters of work rather than by a repetition of one or more of the regular semesters. The retardation will in no case amount to more than four semesters in six years.

5.   (1) The pre-primer class may properly become part of such an organization.

6.   *b.* Dull pupils will spend only six years in the six-year elementary school and will pass on to the junior high school with such knowledge and skills as they have been able to acquire during their six years of attendance.

7. 4. Acceleration and retardation do not depend on certain formulas alone, but are adjustments to individual pupils. From this standpoint, the following policies relative to individual adjustment apply:

8. *a.* Minimum standards for the highest group should be higher than for the lowest or middle group.

9. (1) Fixed standards should not, however, be set for any single section.

10. *b.* Promotion should not be used as a reward for effort or conduct.

11. *c.* Repeating should not be considered except in cases where pupils have failed to reach the standards which they are capable of reaching. Repeating should be used very sparingly then. When the standards have been set beyond the pupils' abilities, the pupils should not be required to suffer.

12. *d.* The Accomplishment Ratio should not be used as a basis for promotion nor for determining the success of a teacher.

13. *e.* Failure because of absence caused by sickness or for other reasons can usually be ruled out unless the child has been away so long that he can, under no circumstance, make up the work missed which is vital to his continuance in school.

14. *f.* All pupils whom the teacher considers unquestionably ready for promotion should ordinarily go ahead.

15. *g.* In all doubtful cases, the educational importance of the subjects in which the deficiency exists should be considered. Different subjects have different promotional values in the different grades, and promotion, subject to a deficiency being made up, may at times well be made.

16. *h.* Promotions should not be based on the results of final tests alone. Rather, observed achievements should be the main factor. A pupil may make a low mark in a written test in one or more subjects, and yet for his own good ought to be promoted.

17. *i.* Ability to do the work of the grade ahead is more important than the attainment of a passing level in that just completed.

18.   *j.* With pupils of average intelligence a year of advanced work is worth more than repeating a grade.

19.   *k.* Repeating a grade is justified when the pupil is unable to master the fundamentals of the succeeding grade because the comparatively small amount of subject matter required cannot be obtained from special instruction given by the new teacher or by a coaching teacher while the pupil carries at least the fundamental work of the following grades.

20.   *l.* Repeating is justified if promotion means the losing of something highly valuable which would not be secured in a higher grade.

21.   *m.* The subject matter lost by going on would need to be of sufficient importance to compensate the boy or girl for the loss that would result from repeating, attention being directed to the fact that for some children repeating a lower grade results in sacrificing the opportunity to secure the experiences of one of the higher grades.

22. 5. If the school is in doubt as to the wisdom of unconditional promotion in a given case the pupil may be conditioned, placed in the next grade, and kept on probation for a period of perhaps six weeks.

23. 6. Repeating, when used, should be limited to not more than one repetition to a grade.

24. 7. When schools have ability grouping, a pupil too low in achievement to go on with his own section may progress with the one just below.

25.   *a.* He may stay in this lower section for the remainder of his school career or, if his difficulties are only temporary, he may return to his original group after a period of recovery.

26.   (1) Coaching at his own level is usually more satisfactory, however, than the plan of putting him in a lower ability group, particularly if he has the native ability of the group above.

II. Promotion in Secondary Schools

27. 1. Secondary schools that promote by grade, undesirable as that is, should pursue the same policies regarding retardation as are suggested for the elementary grades.

28. 2. Pupils should not be failed in try-out courses. The mark given should indicate the quality of the work done but credit should probably be granted, whatever the standard reached.

29. 3. Over-age pupils in junior high school should be advanced to the next level of a required subject if it is felt they have gained about all they are capable of securing in a given level of that subject.

30. 4. Repeating should be permitted only when there is good evidence that it will be more profitable than other courses that might be chosen.

31. 5. In harmony with the principle that credit should be granted if a pupil has reasonably attained the purpose of a course, the following principles may well be adopted:

32. *a.* There are certain courses, such as music, physical education, dramatics and, perhaps, group civics, for which credit is granted for attendance and helpful participation. With respect to repeating, these may be divided into:

33. (1) Those that promise more to a repeater than some new course.

34. (2) Those that give a great deal of their worth the first time to even the poorest participants.

35. (a) In subjects falling in this group, effort put forth in doing the daily tasks assigned must be an important consideration for determining credit.

36. *b.* There are other courses for which credit is granted the pupil when he attains standards in terms of skills, knowledge, or attitudes valuable in themselves. Repeating any subject in this group should be permitted only when mastery of such a subject is required for college entrance, or where the repeating promises greater return than some new subject to be taken in place of it.

37.   (1) Every attempt should be made to get a really objective rating of the pupils' mastery in courses of this type.

38.   c. There are still other courses for which credit is granted the pupil when he attains the skill necessary to carry the next unit of work successfully. Repeating should be required of those who fail if the necessary skill or knowledge is not otherwise readily obtainable. In some cases, as for first-semester algebra, no repeating should be required for failing the term's work, but credit should be granted when the pupil successfully completes the course that follows, just as is the case in annual promotion schools.

39.   (1) The trial promotion plan will often be of service here.

40.   d. There are courses, combining the purposes of (b) and (c), where mastery is required for the sake of the term's work itself, as well as for use in the next course. To determine the desirability of failing, the relative importance of each value must be weighed.

41. 6. Standards for granting credit should vary with the type of course which the pupil is pursuing.

42.   a. If the subject is in the field of the pupil's major interest, or if it is required as preparatory to entrance to a higher institution, the teacher may well hold higher standards than if the subject is taken simply as an informational course.

43.   b. If the planning of a pupil's work demands that a purpose different from the usual one be served by a subject, the standard for granting credit should be different.

44. 7. If a pupil has consciously chosen a course which is beyond his mentality, it is entirely in keeping with the principles govern-

ing the use of retardation that he spend time in addition to the normal amount needed in mastering the course.

45. 8. If a child in the upper grades or junior high school is significantly below the level of his class, he should not be promoted in the tool subjects but should be advanced in the prevocational work if it is seen that he might otherwise drop school at the end of the compulsory age level.

III. ACCELERATION

46. 1. Some data have been collected indicating that nervousness may be aggravated by acceleration. Should any evidence to this effect be found, acceleration for that pupil may well be considered a doubtful procedure.

47. 2. Belief is common that unless a child is actually retarded in social and physiological maturity, as much as one or two years of acceleration in the first six grades and two or three years during the whole twelve may be permitted.

48. 3. A pupil of normal age should not have more than one double promotion a year nor more than two in three years, even though he is shown to have mentality that fits him for more rapid acceleration.

49. 4. The pupil should be accelerated during whatever year in his school career conditions warrant such action, although subject matter and skills which, because of acceleration, have not been secured in the lower grades are usually more readily made up than those lost through acceleration in the upper grades.

50. 5. Skipping should usually come by the middle of the semester, or of the year, if there is annual promotion. Thus the pupil will have a sufficient length of time in the grade to which he is promoted to overcome the handicap caused by skipping and to place himself in full readiness for the following promotion.

51. 6. Only those children should be doubly promoted who, it is felt, will be promoted the following semester.

52. 7. Acceleration may be brought about either by means of high speed sections or through skipping.

53. 8. Although acceleration depends largely on a study of individual cases, yet the superior third of a typical elementary school, excluding the most immature socially and physically, may, without harm, be permitted to finish six years in five. Thus a group adaptation will be brought about.

54.   9. Acceleration under an individual instruction system should be regulated to meet the needs of individual boys and girls.

55.   10. Enrichment is one of the major purposes of acceleration, although enrichment by other means and in varying degrees is sometimes feasible.

56.   *a.* Outside activities, such as music lessons provided by the home, may to a certain extent relieve the necessity of acceleration for purposes of enrichment.

57.   11. Among the types of pupils who should be accelerated for purposes other than primarily for enrichment, are the following:

58.   *a.* Over-age and dull boys and girls who will drop out of school as soon as the law permits.

59.   *b.* Others who may stay on longer but who will eventually be forced out by economic pressure.

60.   *c.* Some who will be able to finish training for a learned profession, provided the total period of training may be finished while they are reasonably young. For such pupils as are achieving on a level that indicates partial mastery of the grade ahead the school probably has no choice but to accelerate.

61.   (1) Even though a pupil can complete his professional course whether he is accelerated or not, he should be considered for acceleration, especially if he plans a considerable amount of graduate study.

62.   *d.* Pupils who began their schooling over-age or who lost schooling because of extended illness should be accelerated until they approach normal age for their grade, provided, of course, there is reasonable assurance that they will succeed in the following grade.

63.   (1) Over-ageness can most certainly be largely overcome if there are well sectioned classes.

64. *e.* Pupils, over-size and physiologically maladjusted, are often just as seriously in need of acceleration as are those who are over-age.

IV. Policies Relative to Acceleration Particularly Applicable to the Elementary School

65. 1. Over-age pupils who are one-half year or more above the standard for their present grade should be advanced.

66. 2. Pupils large for their grade who are one-half year or more above the standard for their present grade should be advanced.

67. 3. Pupils who are one year or more above the standard for the grade they are in should probably be advanced unless already seriously under-age.

68. 4. Even though brightness does not result in high standards of work the bright pupils should probably be accelerated, provided enrichment has been used to the fullest extent, but still the pupil does not have enough to do.

69. 5. Many children who started to school at seven or eight years or older should be considered for double promotion.

70. 6. Many children who have lost schooling because of illness should be given a double promotion.

71. 7. Troublesome cases should be looked up as to intelligence level and character of their daily work. Skipping may remove the disciplinary difficulties.

72. 8. No pupil should be given a double promotion whose educational age does not exceed the lower quartile of the grade to which it is proposed to skip him.

73. 9. No pupil whose E. Q. is below the typical E. Q. of the school should be permitted to skip unless his educational age exceeds the median of the grade.

74. 10. Some pupils who are above grade standards in their tool subjects will be able to skip a grade even though they have less than average intelligence.

75. 11. If the grades are well sectioned, the ability of the pupil to progress after acceleration must be given most serious consideration.

V. ACCELERATION PROBLEMS PECULIAR TO THE SECONDARY SCHOOLS

76. 1. Such experimental evidence as is available tends to show that acceleration of students in the secondary school who demonstrate high ability but who are physically and socially normal or accelerated, does not permanently impair their scholastic standing.

77. 2. Acceleration is by no means as necessary for those who, although otherwise candidates for acceleration, are carrying more than the normal number of outside activities.

78. 3. Acceleration should rarely, if ever, lead to graduation from high school at an earlier age than fifteen or sixteen.

79. 4. The pupil who is to graduate in less than the normal time may have to complete the basic courses in less than the normal time. He may have to take at the same time two courses in English or in mathematics or in the social sciences.

80. 5. Methods by which acceleration may be attained are:

81.   *a.* Permitting the pupils to take courses in excess of the usual number or to enter high speed sections.

82.   (1) High speed sections may be regularly organized or perhaps organized only when it is possible to bring together an especially able group of students.

83.   *b.* Occasionally allowing a pupil who shows himself to be unusually able in a subject to skip the elementary phases of it after he has given satisfactory proof of mastery.

84.   (1) Whether or not credit should be given for this work skipped must be settled by each school.

85.   *c.* In elementary schools where promotion by grade still persists in the seventh and eighth grades, acceleration may be achieved by skipping a whole grade or semester.

86.   *d.* Pupils for whom acceleration is desirable may devote the normal number of years to their high school work, but may earn an excess of credits which will give them advanced standing in college.

87.   *e.* Pupils may be allowed to work ahead in their classes, if they show unusual ability and interest. As soon as they achieve on a level equivalent to the standard for the class just above they will move ahead.

88.   6. The same considerations hold for acceleration in the upper years of public schooling as hold in the lower years.

VI. AGE OF ENTRANCE TO KINDERGARTEN

89.   1. The number of years a child should spend in kindergarten depends on the type of home environment he has and on the type of environment the school furnishes.

90.   2. The one-year kindergarten is for five-year-old children, the child entering at the regular date of entrance nearest his fifth birthday.

91.   *a.* This means that, for schools having annual promotion, children should enter kindergarten who, on September first, are between four years, six months and five years, six months of age. .

92.   (1) Some schools vary this by setting the age on September first necessary to autumn entrance at four years, nine months to five years, nine months. This, however, delays schooling unduly for one-fourth of the children.

93.   *b.* Schools having semi-annual promotion will admit children at the beginning of the first semester who are between four years, nine months and five years, three months, on September first and will admit children at the beginning of the second semester who are within that age range on March first.

94.   3. Children who are precocious may be entered under-age, perhaps six months under-age, but entrance of those who appear to be dull should probably not be delayed.

95.   4. Extremely nervous children, cripples, deafened, and partially sighted children should come to kindergarten only if better provisions can be made there than in the home and if the normal children with whom these deficient children must associate are not made to suffer unduly.

96.   *a.* There should be greater insistence against the enrollment of neurotics than against the enrollment of any
other type of physical defective.

VII. AGE OF ENTRANCE TO FIRST GRADE

97.   1. Entrance of the average child to the first grade should
come just a year later than entrance to the one-year kindergarten.
That is, children entering under the annual promotion system
should enroll between the ages of five years, six months, and six
years, six months, or perhaps five years, nine months, and six
years, nine months, if the school chooses to delay minimum age of
entrance for three months.   Those entering school semi-annually
would enroll the first semester if their age falls between five years
nine months, and six years three months, on September first and
enroll the second semester if their age falls between the same limits
on March first.

98.   2. Age of entrance to the first grade should be subject to
more revision downward than age of entrance to the kindergarten.
Acceleration may be carried to the point of permitting children
who have a mental age of six years to enter, provided they are
at least five years old chronologically.

99.   *a.* Curriculum factors which have a bearing on the physical, social, and intellectual development of the child
should probably be considered as possible modifiers of
any decision based on mental age alone.

100.   3. Age of entrance to the first grade should probably not
be revised upward, even though the child does not have the abilities that qualify him for the usual first-grade work, unless the first
grade curriculum cannot be revised to suit his capacities.

101.   *a.* First-grade entrance of non-kindergarten children can
be accelerated only as a result of a series of tests.
The school must, of course, forego mature teacher
judgment.

102.   (1) Those above average in ability who are not present to avail themselves of early entrance to the
first grade may receive acceleration later in their
school careers.

VIII. Requirements for Entrance to Junior High School

103. 1. The general principle that should operate in determining entrance to junior high school should be that admission of students should be determined on the basis of maturity and the ability of the pupil to profit by the junior high school work offered, rather than by completion of the sixth grade solely.

104. 2. Pupils should enter the junior high school at not later than thirteen or fourteen years of age.

105. *a.* Accompanying this policy should be a minimum of retardation in the elementary school and appropriate subject matter for the different ability levels in every year of school.

106. *b.* If the physical and the social development of the child are accelerated, earlier than usual entrance to the junior high school should be considered. If the development of those traits is retarded, moderate chronological over-ageness is not so serious.

107. 3. No pupil should be held in the elementary school after he has finished the sixth grade.

108. 4. The elementary school principal should have the right to grant a pupil special promotion to junior high school for special reasons, such as unusually high ability, unusual physical or social development, or financial or vocational needs.

IX. Opportunity for Entering Senior High School
With an Excess of Junior High School
Credits Counted

109. 1. Excess credit earned in junior high school should be counted toward senior high school graduation.

110. 2. Pupils ready for 10B work in any subject or those who are deficient in certain courses not offered by one organization, but obtainable in the other, may be allowed to take work in both junior and senior high school, especially if the two organizations are close enough to make passing back and forth convenient. Such a provision will make unnecessary using junior high school credits toward graduation.

111.   *a.* Senior high schools may offer some ninth-grade work or junior high schools may offer some tenth-grade work and thus make unnecessary a student's attending classes in two institutions the same day.

112.   3. A bright child for whom acceleration is not at present feasible may be given enriched and broadened courses which may, if the need later arises, be used as credit toward earlier graduation.

X. SENIOR HIGH SCHOOL ENTRANCE REQUIREMENTS

113.   1. It should be possible for the pupil who has followed a non-college preparatory curriculum in the junior high school to meet the college entrance requirements of the senior high school; the work of the junior high school should in no respect put any restraint on the methods of work and procedure in the senior high school.

114.   *a.* If the junior high school has found it best, with the consent of the parent, to offer the pupil work calling for a much less than normal level of attainment, the pupil must, when he passes to senior high school, enroll in a course suited to his capacity.

115.   *b.* There is especial reason for the low grade pupil going to senior high school if he will there have the advantage of the type of instructional material to which his capacities are particularly adapted.

116.   2. Usually the pupil who has been in junior high school three years should transfer to the senior high school even though he has not completed the requisite number of credits. He can take such ninth-grade work as he must make up by carrying ninth- and tenth-grade work simultaneously or by carrying work in both schools.

117.   *a.* Even though there are minimum subject requirements for senior high school entrance, those can often be as well secured in the senior high school.

118.   *b.* Retention in the junior high school for more than three years will occasionally be more desirable, depending on physical, vocational, social, and educational

needs. Existence of vocational and educational opportunities in one organization or the other should be given
much weight.

119. *c.* Deficiency in the electives at the time of leaving junior
high school should not mean repeating the same subjects the next year, unless greater benefits would
thereby accrue than would obtain if new experiences
were offered.

120. 3. Pupils should be admitted to the senior high school on
the recommendation of the principal of the junior high school from
which they come, even though regular entrance requirements
have not been met.

XI. Senior High School Graduates

121. 1. Colleges should admit on the basis of eleven or twelve
senior high school units.

122. *a.* Such a standard for entrance will permit the junior
high school greater freedom in placing the needs of
the child first.

123. 2. Colleges can safely admit, toward satisfying entrance requirements, a considerable percentage of non-academic high school
work; perhaps, if even fifty per cent of the work is in the vocational group such will not interfere with college success. The
quality of work done is of more importance than the kind of work
done, so far as success in college is concerned.

CHAPTER VII

GUIDANCE

I. RELATION OF GUIDANCE TO FUTURE VOCATION

1. 1. The secondary school should fit its students for the trade, business, or advanced education they plan to enter when they leave school.

A. PREPARATION FOR COLLEGE

2. 1. In order to properly equip a student who is preparing for college the school must provide the courses that are definitely required for entrance to the institution in which the student expects to enroll upon graduation.

3.   *a.* If the pupil falls appreciably and for any length of time below the performance level demanded for college entrance he and his parents should be warned, and, if improvement does not follow, the course should be altered.

B. PREPARATION FOR ENTERING VOCATIONS UPON LEAVING SECONDARY SCHOOL

4. 1. Specific training for the future occupation should increase in amount as the time for its use approaches, whereas general training should correspondingly decrease.

5.   *a.* Pupils who drop out at the end of their junior high school career should receive vocational training during the last year or two in school even though the work be general in nature.

6. 2. Those who intend to enter remunerative occupations either before or upon completion of their high school course should receive some form of organized training rather than depend on the wasteful incidental training they would otherwise experience after leaving school.

7.   *a.* Prerequisites for high school graduation need no longer be considered by those who drop out before graduation. The subjects that can best serve each pupil's needs are the ones for which the pupil should enroll.

8.   (1) Less emphasis will generally be placed on the academic school subjects and a more practical and exploratory type of work will be provided. Cultural curricula should to a certain extent be substituted for abstract studies.

9.   *b.* Rather than attempt to specify a certain vocation that the pupil should enter, the school should show the vocational area in which success seems most likely. The final choice must be left to the pupil.

10.   *c.* Music, art appreciation and similar activities will probably be of relatively higher value to those not finishing high school than will advanced work in geometry, algebra or foreign language.

11.   *d.* Any subject which leaves the pupil with a desire to continue cultural education outside school should be given favorable consideration.

12.   3. If it seems desirable to retain a child in a certain school, even though the courses specifically preparatory to the chosen vocation cannot be offered, the school should then seek to develop qualities, aptitudes and abilities that will prove most useful in the future occupation of that boy or girl.

II. OTHER CRITERIA FOR GUIDANCE

A. INTEREST

13.   1. If interest impels a student to seek with determination a certain subject for which he is eligible under school regulations, that study should generally be thrown open, provided the student is told his chances of success.

14.   *a.* Enough flexibility should exist within and among courses to make this possible.

B. INTELLIGENCE

15.   1. Advanced mathematics, advanced natural science and foreign languages are among those courses which should, in general,

be made up of the upper half or even the upper quartile in intelligence.

16.   *a.* In occasional instances pupils may be allowed to take these courses if they are over-age or if they display marked effort, even though their ability falls below the generally accepted minimum.

17.   *b.* The general level of intelligence of the school, the extent to which subject matter is differentiated for different ability levels, and the requirements of the course in which the pupil is enrolled are also modifying factors.

18.   2. Students may be enrolled in courses generally considered below the level of their ability, but when they are so enrolled they should have their work enriched in worth-while manner and to the extent necessary to challenge their powers.

19.   3. Level of intelligence will in part indicate the wisdom of a student's preparing for a certain vocation. If he possesses intelligence near the median of those now engaged in the vocation this indicates that he has one fundamental quality indicative of success in that occupation.

20.   4. Children who are superior in intelligence should generally secure a more thorough general training before specialization begins than those of the lower ranges of ability. This is generally true for all those entering professions.

21.   *a.* The first years of college may even continue the period of exploration for such pupils.

22.   5. The child with an I. Q. of 90 or less often will not go beyond junior high school unless the curriculum is unusually well accommodated to low abilities. For this reason the eighth grade certainly, and additional grades, if he remains in school, should have for him a strong vocational bent.

23.   6. The child with an I. Q. of 100 often will not finish and will hardly ever go beyond high school. Whether he finishes or not, his last two years in school should have a strong vocational trend.

24.   7. The child with an I. Q. of 110 may go beyond high school and, if so, his vocational program should be arranged accordingly.

25. 8. The child with an I. Q. of 120 is college material and, other things being equal, he will enter college.

26. 9. Genuine and continued interest, to a certain extent, indicate success in a subject or course. However, if interest and intelligence point in opposite directions, intelligence should receive major consideration.

27. 10. Determination and perseverance, either of the parent or of the pupil, are powerful modifiers of school expectancy and as such they should receive careful consideration.

28. *a.* The minimum intelligence necessary for college entrance is lower when the parents or pupil or both express strong preference for such a future. A low intelligence minimum should be given more favorable consideration if the pupil takes less than a normal subject load.

29. *b.* The school had best coöperate with the parents so long as there is hope of success, but if it becomes evident that the task is impossible, evidence of their child's failure must bring the parents to see the proper point of view.

30. 11. Those of low ability who are not driven by unusual pressure into college preparatory courses will spend less time upon the academic school subjects and more time upon lines of a more practical sort.

31. 12. Should the counsellor find the school less well prepared to benefit the pupil than actual working conditions would benefit him, employment may be found for the pupil and he may be advised to withdraw from school.

32. *a.* Those who are of such a mentality that they cannot profit by school work of any sort that the community can provide may be excused from school work and placed in jobs best suited to their abilities. Financial needs exert their influence also.

33. (1) Placement in the job should come only after careful and persistent effort has been made to keep the child engaged in worth-while school activities.

C. Grades made in previous work

34. 1. The grades made in previous related work or in more elementary work of the same type should have considerable weight in determining whether a pupil should enroll in certain subject or course.

35.   *a.* The question as to whether previous failure is attributable to lack of interest or lack of ability must be settled.

36.   *b.* Introductory courses, such as general business practice for commercial work, may be used to test the pupils' aptitudes for further and more extensive work of the same type.

37.   *c.* Grades earned in English may probably be used with a considerable degree of assurance as a basis upon which to advise people about entrance to the more exacting types of secretarial work.

D. Prognostic tests

38. 1. Prognostic tests should be used to the extent that their results have proved to be reliable and valid. Tests to determine further need of English and of other tool subjects appear to have sufficient value to make their adoption desirable.

E. The bright girl

39. 1. The bright girl should probably not take up a vocation incompatible with home life. The vocations possessed of this incompatibility are growing constantly fewer as the woman's sphere of activity becomes more extended or more clearly defined.

F. Deficiencies in the fundamentals

40. 1. Remedial work should be given either in regular or in special classes in order to correct the deficiencies of pupils who are weak in the fundamentals.

G. Deficiencies because of failure

41. 1. Oftentimes those who have failed in one or more subjects should have a change in program at the end of the semester. For those not successfully carried, new courses may be substituted or the subject load may be lightened.

42.   *a.* Deficiencies in credits brought about by any readjustment may be made up by remaining longer in school or by taking summer work.

H. Financial difficulties

43.   1. Unless financial assistance can be secured, the child whose parents are poor may be forced into wage earning sooner than would otherwise be necessary.

44.   *a.* If at all possible, the more able pupils who would otherwise drop out early should be provided with financial assistance or with means of supporting themselves by part-time work.

I. Poor appearance and language handicaps

45.   1. The longer the time the school has to correct deficiencies in appearance and in language the less the significance that should be attached to them in deciding on a vocation. The remediableness should also be considered.

J. Physical and health conditions

46.   1. Physical abilities demanded in the vocation which a pupil contemplates entering should be considered in the planning of his program.

47.   2. A student should choose work compatible with his health. For instance, a person with weak lungs should not choose indoor work when the air is close or filled with dust.

48.   3. Serious effort should be made to solve the problem of finding a vocation in which the physically handicapped child can engage on equal terms with those who are not physically handicapped. He should then be trained accordingly.

K. Strong interests and abilities

49.   1. Unusual or highly developed interests should serve as cues for guidance. Ability in art, music, ceramics, dramatics, public speaking, and in many other activities should be considered in planning the child's program.

50.   *a.* Tests of musical ability and achievement may well be used.

51. 2. Special abilities should be developed as a means of providing leisure time activities.

52. 3. For those who are endowed musically there should be training for participation by performance as well as by appreciation. For those less well endowed, appreciation should be our principal objective.

53. 4. Children who are planning neither for college entrance nor for any other occupation may well devote much time to special abilities. Try-out and exploratory courses should be judiciously used in an endeavor to awaken such interests.

III. EXTRA-CURRICULAR ACTIVITIES

54. 1. All pupils should have membership in those organizations, such as the home room, that assist in the government of the school. All should have a voice in the selection of student council representatives.

55. 2. Organizations such as orchestras, glee clubs, dramatic organizations, and debating clubs should admit members through a try-out process.

56.   *a.* The avenue to such activities should be open through other activities that require less skill or through regular classes.

57. 3. Admission to such organizations as do not require specific skills should be based largely on the pupil's desire to enter, provided the activity is of the type that will best serve his particular needs.

58.   *a.* "Black-balling" by students should not be permitted.

59. 4. No pupil who is seriously failing in his work should represent his school in interschool activities. In intramural activities questions of the relation of level of achievement in regular school work to participation in extra-curricular activities must be settled according to the individual merits of the case.

60. 5. The same methods of classification should be used in extra-curricular intramural physical activities as in physical education, provided social maturity and natural inclination of the pupils toward association are given sufficient consideration.

61. 6. Skills displayed in the intramural contests, with the qualification that school work must be above failure, will determine pupil placement in the interschool contests.

62. 7. It is to be expected that students best qualified to lead will fill the places of greatest responsibility and that those less well qualified will hold the minor positions. Care must be taken to see that the most able do not over-engage in extra-curricular activities and that the less able do not fail altogether to participate.

63.   *a.* The pupils should be unobtrusively assisted by means of discussions in discerning the true qualities of leadership.

64.   *b.* Those who are unprepossessing in appearance and unable to command attention, but who will later be leaders, must receive a major share of their training later in their school career.

65. 8. Pupils should be encouraged to diversify their club and other extra-curricular interests if they show any inclination to do so and if the development of new interests seems desirable.

66. 9. Pupils will generally select as extra-curricular activities those things they can do best. This should generally be viewed with favor since the further development of what one can already do best is a desirable adjustment to individual differences.

67. 10. Those who have a strong desire to enter something new and others who seem to have no active interests should be encouraged to enter fields of activity with which they are not so well acquainted.

68. 11. Extra-curricular activities may be used as a means of correcting deficiencies, provided the spontaneity that results from real interest and self-initiation is maintained and the progress of the group is not unduly retarded by weaklings. Means to be used in achieving this goal are:

69.   *a.* The adviser will arouse interest in the student sufficient to cause him to take up what is best for him.

70.   *b.* Groups of pupils engaged in the various activities will be, so far as possible, classified according to the degree of skill they possess in each particular activity.

CHAPTER VIII

ADJUSTMENT WITHIN CLASSES

I. GENERAL

1. 1. There is abundant evidence that proper adjustment as to organization, course, class or advancement level is insufficient. Adaptations within the classroom are also necessary.

2.   *a.* The work of the individual must be diagnosed to the point where his difficulties are clearly appreciated.

3.   *b.* Oftentimes the variation of the individual from the average will show what additional adjustments are necessary.

4.   *c.* The high school, as well as the grade school, should make a study of each pupil's present attainments and present stage of intellectual maturity, and thus strive to relate its own operations to the pupil's needs.

5.   *d.* The method of treatment must be decided by all teachers, not by one alone.

6.   *e.* The A. R. or A. Q. is both crude and unreliable as a means of determining the degree of maladjustment of the child to the school.

II. ADJUSTMENT TO LOW ABILITY IN GENERAL

7. 1. With slow groups there should be much emphasis on diagnostic and remedial procedures.

A. AMOUNT OF DRILL

8. 1. Low-ability pupils require more drill than the high-ability pupils to reach a given standard. The work must, of course, be within their ability to achieve.

9. 2. Drill by rote should find a large place in the teaching of reading to children with less than average ability. The aim should be to cause the mastery of a limited amount of material to the point of a fair degree of control.

10. 3. In the teaching of spelling, word drill should be repeated at frequent intervals.

11. 4. Extensive drill is needed in the teaching of handwriting, but it should not continue to the point of fatigue.

12. 5. In English, the establishment of basic facts and principles through habit formation is more effective than attempting extensive use of abstract concepts and proceeding from them to the concrete application of these principles.

13. 6. Much drill and repetition is required for the fixing of skills in arithmetic.

14. 7. In the manual arts, repetition at frequent intervals and over long periods of time is effective in securing skills.

15. 8. Children of low ability should acquire automatic responses to certain stimuli that are left to the judgment of the abler pupils.

16. 9. High school pupils need routine drill in perfecting their learning just as do elementary pupils. Those who are dull form faulty, inaccurate bonds and the only way to overcome such deficiencies is by a greater amount of repetition and drill.

17. 10. When pupils temporarily fall below standards they should achieve, the deficiency should be diagnosed and corrected. There should be drill until a sufficient level of mastery is reached.

18. 11. Children who read less than sixty words a minute and who make two or more errors a minute or who require help as often as twice a minute, profit by formal and intensive reading exercises.

19. 12. Similarly, the slow readers in high school will profit from reading drill.

20. 13. Low-ability students should be supplied to the greatest possible extent with prepared habitual-responses behavior patterns.

B. COMPLEXITY OF ASSIGNMENTS

21. 1. The content, as well as the method, should be adapted to the different levels of ability.

22. 2. Those who fall greatly below the class average should be assigned only the most essential of new material.

23. 3. Tasks assigned dull children should be broken up into short, simple units, carefully presented and illustrated, step by step.

24. 4. Low-ability pupils need more stimulation to keep their attention and interest acute.

25. 5. Low-ability pupils should receive greater numbers of concrete illustrations and should experience the continuous specific application of general principles.

C. Standards of Mastery

26. 1. Lower and simpler standards should be set up for the less able children and reasonable attainment of these standards should be expected of all.

27. 2. Minimum standards should be set for each ability level, these standards to differ according to the native ability of the students, their interests, the extent of their school progress, and the character of their aptitudes and deficiencies.

28. 3. Skills the dull child obtains in the first six years will not be so highly developed, and, although the knowledge will be of much the same character, it should be less extensive.

29. 4. Definite goals should be set that will require reasonable attainment for practically all children.

30. 5. If a child has shortcomings so pronounced as to handicap him in adult life, even in connection with the vocations not particularly demanding the trait, then the teacher should attempt to remove the deficiencies, not, however, at the expense of the fields in which he is especially capable.

31. 6. When a pupil's general standing is good but his achievement is low in one or more subjects, he should be given special aid in the subject or subjects in which he shows special weakness. Particularly will he need special assistance if he is one or more years below his grade or group.

32. 7. Children of average or less than average ability, enrolled by their own request in courses which are beyond their level of ability, must expect to achieve at a satisfactory level even though a longer time is thereby required.

D. AMOUNT OF SUBJECT MATTER

33. 1. Children of low ability may carry a normal load in the subjects in which they are especially apt.

34. 2. Children of less than normal ability in a certain field should be assigned only the simpler of the new materials in that field.

35.   *a.* All must certainly acquire the elements which are absolutely essential to the work of the grade above.

E. AMOUNT OF TIME DEVOTED TO CLASS WORK

36. 1. Pupils low in ability should usually spend more time in ordinary school work than those of greater ability; the time those low-ability students spend in recitation or under direct supervision will often be greater also.

37.   *a.* More time will be spent in acquiring the same amount of subject matter.

III. ADJUSTMENT TO UNUSUAL PROFICIENCY IN ORDINARY SCHOOL WORK

A. GENERAL

38. 1. Exceptionally able pupils should be given work as useful to them as ordinary work is to the ordinary individual.

39. 2. In junior and senior high school less time of the able pupils should be taken for mastery because other aspects of the work are more important.

40. *3.* The unusually bright should be given a stimulating environment.

B. AMOUNT OF DRILL

41. 1. In general, the more able students should be required to attain a higher standard in drill subjects and do it in less time.

42.   *a.* However, the abler pupils whose graduation is to be hastened by acceleration will have but little opportunity to acquire a more extensive mastery of the ordinary fields.

43. 2. Stressing of the mechanics of reading should be avoided with these pupils. Mastery of reading and the acquisition of an enriched vocabulary will come through extended silent reading.

44. *a.* Experimental evidence has shown that pupils who read more than sixty words a minute orally with infrequent errors and comparative independence are retarded by instruction and gain more from intensive silent reading experiences.

45. *b.* Similarly, secondary school pupils who are high in reading ability gain nothing from drill.

46. 3. Routine methods should be used to a minimum extent in spelling. Standards should be higher, though, than for the low-ability student.

47. 4. Drill material that is given in handwriting should, so far as possible, have some inherent interest.

48. 5. There should be sufficient repetition of drill material in arithmetic to insure permanency of retention.

49. 6. A bright child should not drop mathematics, for instance, because he is not so proficient in it as in other subjects. Rather he should continue it because it may be vocationally valuable in later years.

50. 7. Glib, clever, bright children of the superficial type should be especially trained in habits of accuracy and thoroughness.

51. 8. Whenever a pupil has proved himself sufficiently a master of the skills he has set out to acquire, drill should be stopped.

52. 9. Material over which sufficient mastery has been attained at some previous time may be skipped altogether. Decision to take this step will come as a result of diagnostic test results.

53. *a.* There are occasions in secondary school when a pupil has reached such a mastery of a subject, as foreign language or English, as will justify his being permitted to omit the elementary work in the subject.

C. ENRICHMENT OF THE SCHOOL PROGRAM

54. 1. The more able pupils should master work more thoroughly and also do it in less time. Time thus saved, if not taken up by acceleration, may well be used for the following adjustments:

55. *a.* Additional activities should be given a pupil whose brightness score is considerably higher than the median of his section, regardless of his average standing in the school subjects.

56. *b.* Additional activities should be given a pupil whose brightness score is higher than the median of his section, provided his average standing in the school subjects, as determined by achievement tests, is equal to the section average.

57. *c.* Additional activities should be given a pupil whose average standing in school subjects is one year above that of his section.

58. 2. When the pupil is not carrying any outside work there is no choice but to enrich within the school.

59. 3. Enrichment should be provided at any time the need for it appears.

60. *a.* Such adjustments as the omission of subjects, the addition of instrumental music and the giving of intelligence tests may usually be taken care of for the whole semester in laying out a pupil's program.

D. THE ADDITION OF ACTIVITIES AND SUBJECTS WHICH LIE OUTSIDE THE REGULAR CURRICULUM

61. 1. Addition of activities which lie outside the regular curriculum often leads to the use of the following:

62. *a.* Extra-curricular activities, sometimes calling for leadership with considerable responsibility attached.

63. *b.* Valuable home activities.

64. *c.* Outside reading. The pupil may at times be furnished with a set of questions as a means of assisting him in interpretative reading.

65.   *d.* Instrumental lessons.

66.   *e.* Freehand drawing.

67.   *f.* Projects, organized into large units and demanding a high standard of achievement, which reach out into many fields the child would otherwise miss.

68.   *g.* Extra reading assignments in the content subjects or the following of interests in reading; animal stories for some; fairy tales for others; adventure for others.

69. 2. The type of activity chosen should suit the abilities, interests and needs of the boy or girl.

70. 3. Even though the particular talent of a pupil is not well developed, the school should recognize and nourish the potentialities that exist.

E. INCREASE IN THE VARIETY AND NUMBER OF APPLICATION OF PRINCIPLES

71. 1. With more able children, general directions and general questions should be used so far as the pupil can follow them intelligently. In general, the learning situation may be made more complex for the more able pupils.

72.   *a.* Those who differ considerably but not markedly from the average may be cared for by assignments that require different types of application of the work being offered.

73. 2. General principles should be sought out in class discussion. The bright pupils should make a more extensive application of principles than the others.

74. 3. Interference should be used guardedly in order to give the exploring tendency of the pupil a chance to operate with minimum interference.

75.   *a.* There is some danger, though, that the bright children will get too far afield in their discussion. Their attention must then be called to the relevancy of matter under discussion.

76. 4. In the secondary school enrichment will often have to come in one subject—the one best adapted to such treatment.

77. 5. Materials in history and literature that usually belong to higher educational levels or that consist of the more unusual but still worth-while subject matter should be used to enrich the programs of the more able pupils.

78.   *a.* It is to be remembered that enrichment does not consist merely in longer assignments.

79. 6. Solution of hard but valuable problems, and arithmetic puzzles, the reading of biographies of mathematicians, studying the history of mathematics, all may be used in broadening in worthwhile fashion the field of mathematics.

F. STANDARDS OF WORK REQUIRED

80. 1. A higher standard of work should be required of the abler pupils than of others.

81.   *a.* However, those who tend to injure their health and too greatly emphasize the academic phase of school life by carrying their work beyond the level which they should attain must be restrained.

82. 2. The more able pupils in secondary school should often carry a normal number of subjects with adjusted assignments in one or more subjects. These adjustments should require a more complete mastery, a broader field of knowledge and a more extensive application of principles.

IV. CORRECTION OF TEMPORARY DEFICIENCIES IN SCHOOL SUBJECTS

83. 1. Pupils given or to be given a special promotion should receive special help according to the nature of the work skipped. Whether this corrective work is given before or after double promotion depends on the period elapsing between the time of realization that a special promotion is desirable and the time the promotion should be consummated.

84.   *a.* Make-up work used to bring a specially promoted pupil up to grade will serve for a time as enrichment material.

85. 2. Work missed because of absence or only partially mastered because of failure should be made up at the earliest opportunity.

86. *a.* Many pupils who passed conditionally will be able to master the work of the next grade if special instruction is given.

87. *b.* Adjustments should be made for children who are older both physiologically and chronologically than others in their class and who have been held back by ill-health, or foreign tongue or by lack of training. Likewise they should not be held to a common course of study.

88. 3. When deficiencies exist in subjects which are no longer provided in the regular curriculum, these subjects may be handled as auxiliary activities in one of the regular classes. For example, reading, spelling, language usage, and penmanship may be given in high school English classes. Improvement may at other times be brought about by direct instruction in remedial classes.

89. 4. Reading deficiencies which are the foundation of much difficulty in other subjects should be corrected. This should be done even when reading is no longer taught.

90. *a.* Some poor readers need training in avoiding repetition; others, training in paying attention to content.

91. *b.* Assignments that require him to read carefully for the answers to specific questions should be used to break down a pupil's habit of jumping at conclusions without verifying them.

V. Adjustment to Special Abilities and Disabilities Outside Regular School Work

A. Special abilities

92. 1. Provision should be made for pupils with special abilities, such as those in music, plastic art, painting, drawing, expression, dancing, sketching, building of models, and research in science such as radio.

93. *a.* The pupil who is not able to participate successfully in singing should be considered as to the possibility of his becoming a member of the school orchestra or even participating in the making of simple musical instruments.

94.   *b.* The fact that a child is bright is not conclusive evidence that he can profit most by music, art and foreign languages. The interests of the gifted will be found to vary enormously and the school must make provision for the variation.

B. SPECIAL DISABILITIES

95. 1. The school should stress such social adjustments as the following:

96.   *a.* Children who are too timid to enter into play activities should be reasonably encouraged to do so.

97.   *b.* Service to the group should be required of those who are selfish and unwilling to give and take.

98.   *c.* Brilliant pupils who are learning to lead selfish lives should be taught the proper attitudes.

99.   *d.* The child should be counselled concerning personal habits which place him in an unfavorable light before others.

100.   *e.* Those who have volitional patterns that are predisposed against school should be led to see themselves as others see them and to realize that school offers the opportunities which they should take advantage of and be willing and anxious to enjoy.

101.   *f.* Deficiencies in the knowledge of how to comport oneself at the table and in other social situations, including how to meet people, should be remedied.

102.   *g.* Little children should learn desirable social attitudes and habits as early in life as possible.

103. 2. The school should see defects in children's appreciation of the æsthetics and should remove the deficiencies.

104.   *a.* Music and art should be made meaningful.

105.   *b.* Utilization of leisure time to best advantage should be taught.

106. 3. Health will determine the type of program that is to be furnished, as well as the load which the pupils will carry and the amount of acceleration he will be allowed if he is otherwise able.

CHAPTER IX

CORRECTIVE CLASSIFICATION OF INDIVIDUAL PUPILS

I. Adjustment Relative to Organizations and Curricula

A. General

1. 1. Pupils should be periodically appraised, say, at classification time, each semester. This will constitute an administrative procedure that will aid flexibility.

2. 2. School organization should be sufficiently flexible to allow for shifting among groups for instruction, commensurate with the relative gain or loss in ability on the part of certain individuals.

B. Adjustment in courses

3. 1. Factors are continually arising which make it imperative that guidance shall not be limited to the junior high school period. Factors which may change are:

4. *a.* Home conditions.

5. *b.* Other environmental conditions.

6. *c.* Intensity of stimuli prompting a child to pursue a certain course.

7. 2. A pupil's course, once selected, should not be considered so definitely settled that only failure or choice of the pupil or parent result in a modification.

8. 3. If it is the school's fault that a child has been misdirected, the course of the pupil should be altered. If it is the pupil's fault, he should become a case for careful clinical investigation.

9. 4. A pupil in senior high school should be permitted and encouraged to change his course whenever it seems best.

10. *a.* A minimum penalty should be exacted by way of loss of credits.

11. *b.* The sequential study of certain subjects in order to obtain their maximum value must be considered.

12. 5. The counsellor should prevent transfers caused by maladjustments which might be remedied.

13. 6. The counsellor should encourage transfer when, obviously, abilities and requirements are not being adjusted.

14. 7. There should be no loss by transfer in any course except where such loss in necessary to obtain the really basic training in the field the pupil later chooses.

15. 8. Short commercial courses in high school should not be barriers to those who find themselves able to remain in school and continue their education after completing the course.

C. CORRECTIVE ADJUSTMENT IN GRADE OR ADVANCEMENT LEVEL

16. 1. School organization should be sufficiently flexible to allow shifting at any time to correct errors in classification.

17. *a.* Rapid increase in the diversity of groups makes this plan necessary.

18. 2. Special promotions *ad interim* should be trial promotions, with the policy of quick return to a lower grade if too much is being attempted.

19. 3. In the case of trial promotion, there should be a definite probationary period of six weeks or so followed by a formal and recorded decision.

20. 4. Promotion within the year or the semester should always be a possibility for the industrious pupil.

21. 5. Any pupil, not promoted at a regular promotional time, should have the right to appeal to the principal.

22. *a.* Objective tests should be used to settle the question.

23. 6. Ability groups within a class should shift from day to day, depending on a pupil's particular stage of development.

24. 7. If a child in a class with mental subnormals at any time shows the ability to do work with the regular class, he should be taken from the class for subnormals and transferred to a regular class group.

25. 8. Each teacher should periodically and continuously consider the possibility of extra promotion of certain members of her class.

D. CORRECTIVE ADJUSTMENT IN ABILITY GROUPS

26. 1. In the secondary school transfer should be made freely from one ability group to another as evidence of misplacement appears.

27. 2. Whenever ability grouping is used, the more frequently articulation points can be found the better, because transfers can thus be made without loss to any pupil.

28. 3. It is not advisable to use shifting from section to section in lieu of promotion. Such movement should occur only when it is discovered that a pupil has been placed in the wrong brightness or mental ability group.

29. 4. The group test should not be considered as a final or sole criterion in making permanent classification of groups.

E. VARIATION IN THE CURRICULUM CONTENT

30. 1. There should be diagnosis of curriculum content as investigation shows it to be necessary.

II. CLASSIFICATION OF NEW PUPILS

31. 1. When a child ten to twelve years of age enters school for the first time he should be placed in an ungraded room until he attains at least second grade reading ability.

32.   *a.* If an ungraded room is not available, he should be placed with children near his chronological age if he has normal intelligence, and be assigned to the first grade for reading. His classification should not be fixed for a half year or so.

33. 2. Pupils who come in from outside schools should be placed in the grade or section that their achievement and past record seem to warrant.

34.   *a.* Proper allowance should be made for difference in type of preparation.

35. 3. Every child who transfers from another school system should be given tests in the various subjects as a means of determining the grade in which he should be placed.

36. 4. The placement of pupils in the regular grades upon being discharged from physical disability classes should be determined by means of achievement tests, intelligence tests and a physical examination.

CHAPTER X

DATA NECESSARY FOR ADEQUATE CHILD ACCOUNTING

The data presented in this chapter in summary form are only those that are necessary for the adequate operation of the policies stated in the preceding chapters. The data were obtained by analyzing each policy and combining the results. The method used may be illustrated by reference to policies 1 and 2 in Chapter II. These policies state:

1. 1. The upper intelligence limit for entrance to a class for mental subnormals should be an I. Q. of 75 or 80. The lower limit should be an I. Q. of 50 or 55, with the provision that children showing a distinct foreign language handicap may enter with an I. Q. as low as 45.
2.   *a.* The I. Q. obtained from a group test should be confirmed by at least one individual intelligence test, given by a competent examiner.

Data needed for the adequate operation of these policies are found by inspection to be those shown in Table I.

A table similar to Table I was made for the analysis of all policies in Chapters II to IX, inclusive.[1] The data required by each of the policies were then combined. As stated in Chapter I, these data were found to classify themselves under two general heads, namely, those regarding the individual pupil and those regarding the adjustment made by the school to that pupil.

The summary also revealed the period throughout the individual's life during which the information should be secured, and the specific group of individuals concerning whom it should be secured. Oftentimes one policy called for the collection of a particular item for all pupils over a certain period and another policy demanded the collection of the same data during the remainder of their school career. Other data were found to be

---

[1] These tables are on file, with other manuscript material, in the library of Teachers College, Columbia University.

TABLE I

DATA NEEDED FOR THE ADEQUATE OPERATION OF POLICIES ONE AND TWO
IN CHAPTER II

POLICY NUMBER	CONCERNING WHOM	DATA REGARDING THE INDIVIDUAL PUPIL		DATA RELATIVE TO SCHOOL ADJUSTMENT
		Item	When Obtained	
I	All	I. Q. (group)	As soon as determinable	Whether in regular class or in class for mental subnormals
	Same	Foreign language handicap	Same	
2	Same	I. Q. (group)	Same	Same
	Those tentatively selected for classes for mentally subnormal	I. Q. (indiv.)	When group tests indicate low I. Q.	

needed only for certain types of individuals or for certain periods, as during the pupil's high school career.

Some decision was necessary in regard to time and frequency of gathering data. It seemed reasonable to assume that data regarding the individual himself should be gathered at the time the data are obtainable and as frequently as changes occurred which were significant in adjusting the school to the child. Data relating to school adjustment should probably be recorded at the time the adjustment is made.

Certain school adjustments are made day by day. These, if recorded, should appear on a day-to-day record. Other adjustments occur less frequently and may well appear on either general or specialized permanent cumulative records. As specialized records increase in frequency the general records will decrease in importance and in the amount of data they contain. Only a few of the possible specialized records are suggested.

Although only occasional reference has been made to the type of record on which data regarding the individual should appear, this may be determined from a consideration of several factors, such as: (1) Concerning whom the data are to be obtained; (2) when in the individual's life or school career they are to be obtained; and (3) how frequently they are to be obtained.

The items on the succeeding pages certainly do not include all data needed for child accounting. Group adjustments, as well, must receive consideration. Other information must probably be obtained in order that the school census may be adequately maintained. Still other information is needed in order to insure satisfactory attendance. Some data are perhaps needed purely for historical purposes. It is, nevertheless, the belief of the author that by far the greatest percentage of the information necessary to a system of child accounting is listed in this chapter.

I. DATA CONCERNING THE INDIVIDUAL

A. To Be Obtained from All.

1. Statement of health and physical conditions, including in the latter classification statements as to severity, and whether defects are remediable or non-remediable. (To be obtained at time of physical examination and when change is observed, beginning with those being considered for entrance to kindergarten.)

   II: 6, 27; III: 2-4, 70, 72, 79, 89, 120; IV: 20, 39, 49, 55; V: 17, 21, 29; VI: 99, 100, 118; VII: 47, 48; VIII: 81, 106, 107; IX: 36.

   a. Past and present diseases and illnesses that might influence present abilities and needs, including:
      III: 81; VI: 13, 62, 70; VIII: 87.

      (1) Tuberculosis now arrested or cured.
          III: 78.
      (2) Record of epileptic attacks.
          III: 1, 119.

   b. Present diseases and illnesses, including:
      III: 81; VI: 13, 62, 70; VIII: 87.
      (1) Headaches.
          III: 38.
      (2) Nervousness.
          III: 38, 79, 83, 106; VI: 46, 95, 96.
      (3) Progressive or chronic catarrhal condition.
          III: 59.

(4) Active pulmonary tuberculosis.
III: 74.

(5) Exposed to open case of tuberculosis at present or recently.
III: 76.

(6) Closed tuberculosis in any organ without known exposure.
III: 77.

(7) Anemia, malnutrition, continual tired feeling.
III: 79, 80.

(8) Frequency of colds.
III: 79.

(9) Epilepsy.
III: 1, 119.

(10) Cardiac diseases and extent, it being specified whether potential or congenital.
III: 5, 8, 82, 90, 93, 95, 96.

c. Degree of convalescence. (Continually while ill.)
III: 7, 81.

d. Existing deficiencies or handicaps and severity of.

(1) Visual acuity. (In better eye after refraction.)
III: 1, 17, 23, 24, 26, 29, 30, 33, 37, 40-42; VI: 95.

(a) Oculist's opinion as to need for sight-saving classes.
III: 34, 37.

(b) Specific types of eye defects and severity of.
Consider: Secondary cataracts, whether acute or not, squinting; congenital cataracts, and whether acute or not; symptoms of asthenopia, frowning, inactive keratitis, diopters of astigmatism, trachoma, extent of corneal opacities, blepharitis, hyperopia, diopters of myopia, whether progressive or not; lachrymation, congenital malformation or fundus lesions and whether acute or not; evidence of eye fatigue.
III: 17, 18, 21, 24, 27-33, 37-39.

(2) Auditory acuity. (Measured according to audiometer and according to ability to hear speech.)
III: 1, 44, 48, 53-58, 60, 66, 114; IV: 39; VI: 95.

(a) Type of deafness, including:
III: 66.

(1) Nerve deafness.
III: 59.

(2) Congenital deafness.
III: 47.

(b) Sit to favor hearing.
III: 45.

(c) Cotton in ear.
III : 45.
(d) Possibility of conserving remaining hearing.
III : 66.
(3) Malformation of speech organs.
III : 107, 110, 111.
(a) Type of speech defects.
III : 101-117; IV : 39.
(1) Severity of.
III : 105-108.
(2) Organic or inorganic.
III : 101-117.
(4) Crippling deformities, specified and severity of :
III : 6, 8-12, 14, 15, 87; VI : 95.
(a) Active or inactive.
III : 6, 8-12, 14, 15, 87.
(b) Ability in locomotion.
III : 6, 8-12, 14, 15, 87.
(5) Left-handedness.
III : 118.
e. Size for grade, height and weight—change in these qualities being noted.
II : 13; III : 79, 85, 86; VI : 64, 66.
(1) Per cent under-weight.
III : 84.

2. Home environment—general desirability. (To be determined periodically and as information becomes available.)
III : 49, 127; VI : 56, 89, 95; IX : 4.
a. Language in the home.
VIII : 87.
b. Economic pressure in the home and on the student.
IV : 23; VI : 59-61, 108; VII : 32, 33, 44.
c. Outside work carried.
VIII : 58.
d. Determination and perseverance of parents in advocating certain courses and vocations.
VII : 27.

3. Pupil's interests, including major interest. (Periodically and as information becomes available.)
III : 13; IV : 32; V : 17; VI : 42; VII : 49, 68, 69; VIII : 27, 69, 94.
a. Interests in specified subjects, fields and courses, including those in which previously failed.
VII : 13, 26, 35.

b. Type of vocation for which preparation is desired.
III: 21; IV: 17; VII: 1.

c. Determination and perseverance of child in urging certain courses and vocational preparation.
VII: 27.

4. Abilities, aptitudes and attitudes. (Those subject to continuous significant change to be recorded continually; others periodically and when change is noted.)

   a. Social qualities.

   (1) Social maturity.
   II: 31; V: 4, 29; VI: 47, 53, 76, 99, 100, 106, 108; VII: 60.

   (2) Traits of glibness and cleverness.
   VIII: 50.

   (3) Timidity in regard to entering into school activities.
   VIII: 96.

   (4) Achievement in social attitudes and habits, including unselfishness, and willingness to give and take.
   V: 38; VIII: 97, 98, 102.

   (5) Seriousness and specific character of unattractiveness, deficiencies in appearance and undesirable personal habits, including deficiencies in table manners.
   VII: 45, 64; VIII: 99, 101.

   b. Qualities of leadership.
   V: 38; VII: 62, 64.

   (1) Probable opportunity for leadership later.
   VII: 64.

   c. Measures of native ability.

   (1) M. A. (Group.)
   II: 9; III: 17, 72, 89; IV: 45; V: 4; VI: 98, 101, 102; VIII: 4.

   (2) I. Q. (Group.)
   II: 1, 2, 8, 11, 28, 33, 41, 42, 44, 45; III: 104, 109; IV: 20, 21, 43; V: 10, 13, 15, 20, 22, 24-26, 28, 30, 37, 40, 55, 61; VI: 2-6, 8, 9, 11, 18, 19, 24, 26, 29, 44, 49, 53, 58, 63, 68, 71, 74-77, 82, 99, 100, 112; VII: 15-26, 28, 30-33, 39; VIII: 7, 8, 21, 22, 27, 32, 33, 38; IX: 29, 32, 36.

   (3) C. A.
   II: 12-15, 30-32, 41; III: 13, 27; IV: 18, 23, 30, 31, 33, 46, 47, 50, 57; V: 19, 25, 28; VI: 1, 29, 48, 62, 65, 67, 70, 77, 78-94, 97, 98, 101, 102, 104, 106; VII: 16; VIII: 87, 106; IX: 31, 32.

(4) Physiological age or physical maturity.
V: 4, 17; VI: 47, 53, 64, 76, 103, 106, 108; VIII: 87.
d. Measures of traits depending on both native and acquired ability.
(1) E. Q.
V: 13-15, 26, 37; VI: 73.
(2) E. Q. plus I. Q.
VIII: 55, 56.
(3) E. A.
II: 9; III: 72, 89; IV: 45, 47; V: 18; VI: 72, 73.
(4) Aptitudes—general.
II: 18; III: 13; VII: 3, 29.
(a) Those possessed which are requisite to a particular vocation, including physical abilities.
III: 2; IV: 20; VII: 46.
(b) Those necessary for higher education.
VI: 118; VII: 3, 29.
(5) Special abilities or talents, such as those in music, plastic art, painting, drawing, sketching, building of models; research in science, such as radio; expression and dancing and other special abilities.
II: 19; V: 38; VII: 49, 52; VIII: 70, 92-94.
(6) Specific vocational aptitudes and abilities, including abilities and records made in try-out and exploratory courses.
IV: 30; VII: 12, 13, 31-33, 44, 53.
(7) Achievement in appreciation of the æsthetic, in understanding music and art, in the utilization of leisure time.
VIII: 103, 105.
(8) Specific levels of achievement, including deficiencies, level of ability in work skipped, language ability, prognostic test results, school record in other schools attended, work in try-out courses, including enrichment courses.
II: 7, 16, 20-22, 24-30, 32-42, 44; III: 7, 17, 104, 123; IV: 25, 35, 37, 42, 43, 50, 51, 54, 57; V: 11, 12, 22, 25, 31, 32, 39, 41, 42; VI: 2-6, 8, 9, 11, 15-17, 19, 22, 24-26, 28, 29, 36-40, 42, 44, 45, 49, 51, 60, 62, 63, 65-68, 71, 74-77, 83, 87, 108, 114, 119; VII: 18, 29, 31, 35, 38, 40, 44, 45, 50, 52, 55, 59, 68; VIII: 2-4, 7, 14, 16-22, 26-33, 35, 41, 42, 44-49, 51-54, 57, 69, 80, 81, 83-89, 94, 106; IX: 1, 8, 13, 17, 18, 22-25, 27, 33, 35, 36.
(9) Physical abilities.
(a) Strength indices.
V: 44-51, 55, 56; VII: 60.
(b) Stunt scores.
V: 44, 45, 56; VII: 60.

(c) Physical fitness index.

V: 47-50, 55, 56.

(10) Levels of achievement in accuracy and thoroughness.

VIII: 50.

(11) Teacher judgment as to ability to succeed in next higher grade or level; or in grade to which admission by double promotion is considered; or in the grade in which now placed. (When promotion is considered.)

II: 39; V: 13, 15, 16, 26, 27, 37; VI: 14, 17, 29, 51, 62, 75.

(a) Record of appeal made to principal, if not promoted.

IX: 21.

(12) Evidence that repeating will be of more value than other adjustments, such as a new course; also value to be obtained by repetition.

VI: 30, 33, 34, 36, 40, 119.

(13) Facility in the use of English.

II: 1; IV: 33, 34, 43-45, 48.

(14) Adviser's opinion as to vocational area in which success is most likely.

II: 18; VII: 9.

(a) Vocational needs.

VI: 118.

(15) Specific ability in the making of musical instruments. (Continually if engaged in work.)

VIII: 93.

e. Behavior difficulties, including lying, stealing, delinquency and truancy. (As they arise.)

III: 50, 120, 124-126, 132; V: 53; VI: 71.

(1) Volitional patterns predisposed against school.

VIII: 100.

f. Extra-curricular record.

(1) Progress in extra-curricular activities.

VII: 68.

(2) Extra-curricular activities, including leisure time activities, in which pupil can best perform and with which pupil has acquaintance and is interested.

VII: 51, 60, 66, 67.

(a) Positions of leadership held outside of school.

VII: 62.

(3) Skill displayed in extra-academic work both in and out of the curriculum, such as sports, orchestra, glee club, dramatics, debating, art, all music, ceramics, public speaking.

VII: 49, 55, 56, 61, 70.

(4) Specific extra-curricular interests, including inclination to diversity and those activities pupils desire to enter, including also inter-school sports and intra-mural sports.
VII: 57, 59, 60, 65, 67.

(5) Evidence of need for new extra-curricular interests.
VII: 65.

(6) Specific deficiencies subject to correction by means of extra-curricular activities.
VII: 69.

g. General industry and energy displayed, in curricular and extra-curricular activities. (Periodically or when special promotion is planned.)
II: 27; V: 17; VI: 35; VII: 16; IX: 20.

(1) Fields in which self-initiation is most pronounced.
VII: 68.

5. Future plans. (Periodically and as information becomes available.)

a. Further training planned to pursue, including night school, names of institutions and their prerequisites for admission being secured.
IV: 18, 19, 23, 38; VI: 2, 21, 36, 42, 58, 59, 61; VII: 1, 2, 5-8, 10, 11, 23-25, 29, 30, 44, 53.

b. Occupations planned to enter, both with and without advisory assistance.
III: 13; IV: 22, 30, 41; VI: 60, 108; VII: 4, 6, 9, 12, 19-25, 30, 31, 36, 37, 39, 44, 46-48.

6. Vocation in which engaged, part or full time. (Periodically and as information becomes available.)
IV: 24, 29, 30, 40.

B. *To Be Obtained from Those Above the Elementary School Level.*

1. Measures of physical maturity. (Periodically.)

a. Dentition age.
V: 29.

b. Weight age.
V: 29.

c. Height age.
V: 29.

d. Normal strength for age and weight.
V: 47-50.

2. Record of class participation—helpful or otherwise. (Continu-

ally for those enrolled in music, physical education and group civics.)

VI: 32-34.

3. Environmental factors other than the home. (Periodically.)

IX: 5.

4. Intensity of stimuli acting on the pupils. (Periodically.)

IX: 6.

5. Attitude toward school work. (Periodically.)

V: 30.

6. Specific levels of achievement in attitudes. (Continually for those above elementary school level enrolled in subjects in which attitudes are high in importance.)

VI: 36, 37.

7. Data relating to secondary school entrance. (When entrance is considered.)

a. Degree to which entrance requirements are met.

VI: 120.

b. Recommendation of junior high school principal regarding promotion to senior high school.

VI: 120.

8. Choice of subjects and course by pupils and parents. (Periodically.)

VI: 123; VII: 34; IX: 7.

9. Purpose for which subject is taken. (Periodically and as information becomes available.)

V: 35; VI: 42, 43.

10. Strength of preference of parent for college entrance. (Periodically.)

VII: 28.

11. Specific requirements pupils must meet for further schooling, vocation, etc., with indication as to which is basic. (As information becomes available.)

IV: 41; VII: 12; IX: 13, 14.

12. Consent of parent to less than normal level of attainment. (When the junior high school wishes to set lower standards.)

VI: 114.

13. Tenacity. (Periodically.)

V: 30.

14. Æsthetic intelligence. (Periodically.)

V: 38.

15. Mechanical ability. (Periodically.)

V: 38.

16. Ability in creative writing. (Periodically.)

V: 38.

17. Social group of which a member. (Periodically.)
V: 27.

18. Preference as to attendance at summer school. (When entrance is being considered.)
IV: 57.

C. *To Be Obtained from Those Who Are Deafened.* (*Periodically and when change is noted.*)

1. Ability in learning speech.
III: 52.

2. Ability in reading.
III: 60-62.

3. Indications of eyestrain.
III: 67.

4. I. Q. (Individual.)
III: 50.

5. Home conditions as related to suitableness of upbringing.
III: 49.

6. Accessibility of the home to the day school for deafened children.
III: 51.

7. History of family deafness.
III: 58.

8. Attitude toward own deafness.
III: 66.

D. *To Be Obtained from Those Who Have Speech Difficulties.* (*At time of physical examination and when change is noted.*)

1. Inhibition of normal activity in presence of normal children.
III: 105.

2. Embarrassment caused by defect.
III: 105.

3. Foreign influences in the environment. (From those with foreign substitutions in speech sounds.)
III: 116.

4. Diseases of childhood. (From those with sluggish enunciation.)
III: 117.

5. Character of muscular coördination.
III: 117.

E. *To Be Obtained from Those in Fresh Air Classes.* (*At frequent intervals.*)

1. Amount of sleep secured at home.
III: 69.

2. Kind of food obtained at home.
   III: 69.
3. Deficiencies that brought the child into the fresh air class.
   III: 88.

F. *To Be Obtained from Those with Potential Cardiac Diseases. (At time of the physical examination and when change is noted.)*

1. Does the pupil have tonsilitis, myositis, recurring chorea (Severity of?) joint pains, growing pains, heart murmurs, definite valvular lesions, history of acute rheumatism?
   III: 97-100.

G. *To Be Obtained from Those with Cardiac Difficulties Who Are Too Ill to Attend School. (At time of leaving school and periodically until returned.)*

1. Residence address.
   III: 92.
2. Character of illness.
   III: 92.

H. *To Be Obtained from Those Who Are Exceptionally Able, Whether in Classes for Gifted Children or Not. (Periodically, and when entrance to special class is given consideration.)*

1. I. Q. (Individual.)
   V: 20, 21.
2. Extent to which well occupied by school work.
   VI: 68.
3. Teacher's judgments as to effort child will display in special classes.
   V: 22.
4. Distance of class for gifted from pupil's home.
   V: 21.
5. Need for enrichment.
   VI: 55, 56.

I. *To Be Obtained for Those in or Being Considered for a Class for Mental Subnormals. (Periodically.)*

1. I. Q. (Individual.)
   II: 2, 4, 11, 13; III: 41, 44.
2. I. Q. (Individual retest.)
   II: 5, 7.
3. Judgment of teachers, principal and supervisor as to ability to succeed in regular class.
   II: 3.

4. Further observation of teacher, principal and supervisor as to ability to succeed in regular class. (To be obtained if first judgment is favorable.)
II: 3.

5. Judgment of special teacher as to necessity for remaining in special class.
II: 7.

J. To Be Obtained from Those Too Low to Profit by a Class for Mental Subnormals. (When group and individual tests indicate the advisability of exclusion.)

1. Consent of the parents to placing the child in a special institution.
II: 4.

2. Judgment of teacher, principal and supervisor as to necessity for exclusion.
II: 5.

3. I. Q. (Individual retest.)
II: 5, 7.

K. To Be Obtained from Those for Whom a Clinical Study Is Necessary. (At time the study is made.)

1. Results of the psychiatrical or psychological study or both.
III: 120.

2. Psychopathic difficulties, including temper tantrums.
III: 128, 129, 131.

3. Record of results of consultations with specialists.
III: 129.

4. Record of sex difficulties, epilepsy, chorea, stuttering, stammering, chronic truancy, dementia præcox or over-protection in the home.
III: 133-138.

L. To Be Obtained from Those Being Considered for Kindergarten Entrance. (At time entrance is being considered.)

1. Evidence of precocity or dullness such as I. Q. according to a group intelligence test.
VI: 94.

2. Probable influence on normal children, if inclined to be abnormal or subnormal.
VI: 95.

M. To Be Obtained from Those Being Considered for Junior High School Entrance. (When entrance is under consideration.)

1. Recommendation of elementary school principal as to promotion.
VI: 108.

2. Ability to profit by junior high school work. (Opinion of teacher, also other bases.)
VI: 103.

N. To Be Obtained from Those in or Being Considered for Afternoon or Evening Classes. (When entrance is being considered.)

1. Citizenship and vocational requirements they are seeking to meet.
IV: 34.
2. Degree of literacy.
IV: 33, 34.
3. Country of birth.
IV: 33.
4. Desire as to leaving or continuance in present vocation.
IV: 40.
5. Purpose for which course is taken. (To be obtained periodically.)
IV: 43.
6. Specific requirements pupils must meet for further schooling, vocation, etc., with indication as to which are basic.
IV: 41.
7. Length of time expecting to continue night school.
IV: 41.

O. To Be Obtained from Foreign Mothers. (Periodically.)

1. Contacts with English speaking groups.
IV: 36.

P. To Be Obtained from Those in Continuation School. (Periodically.)

1. Evidence of misfit in industry in which engaged.
IV: 25.
2. Specific vocational aptitudes and abilities.
IV: 25.

Q. To Be Obtained from Those Who Are Seeking Admission as Indentured Apprentices. (At entrance and when status changes.)

1. Acceptance by employer as an indentured apprentice.
IV: 27.

R. To Be Obtained from Those Who Are Seeking Admission as Coöperative Students. (At the time of entrance and when their status changes.)

1. Acceptance by employer on a coöperative basis.
IV: 28.
2. Specific vocational aptitudes and abilities.
IV: 28.

II. Data Regarding School Adjustment

A. To Be Obtained for All.

1. General data for the permanent cumulative record.
   a. Age at which began school.
      VI: 62, 69.
   b. Date of entrance each year or semester.
      II: 24.
   c. Record of attendance and absence, including date school career is terminated.
      II: 24; IV: 29, 42; VI: 13, 32; VIII: 85.
   d. Years attendance at school.
      II: 11; IX: 16, 17, 25.
   e. Record, including time awarded, of all promotions and non-promotions—regular, double, conditional, revoked conditional and finally approved conditional.
      II: 25; IV: 51-53, 56; VI: 22, 38, 39, 50, 121, 122; VIII: 86; IX: 7, 18-22.
   f. Record of planned special promotion.
      II: 27.
   g. Work skipped through special promotion and otherwise.
      II: 26; VI: 83; VIII: 52, 53.
   h. Importance of subject matter not covered and not obtainable in next higher grade.
      VI: 20, 21.
   i. Organization in which enrolled, including:
      School in which enrolled, with designation and whether public or private; institution, whether elementary, junior or senior high school or both; kindergarten; departmentalized organization or otherwise; regular or special class and exact type; corrective class and whether full- or part-time; full-time or continuation school; afternoon or evening school; special class in high school; whether special institution or home; hospital provisions; summer school; fresh air class; factory class; parental or truant school, with location indicated; class for indentured apprentices; enrollment in coöperative school; isolation; exclusion.
      II: 1-5, 7-14, 16, 30-39, 41, 42, 45; III: 1, 2, 11, 15, 16, 39, 41, 44, 45, 47-55, 57-59, 68, 71, 73-84, 86-88, 90, 103-106, 119, 121, 127, 128; IV: 23, 27, 28, 32-39, 42, 49-57; V: 3, 27; VI: 89-96, 103, 104, 110, 111, 115, 118; VII: 42; IX: 1, 24, 31-36.
   j. Grade in which enrolled, including organization in which grade work is given.
      II: 9, 11, 32; III: 2, 3, 10, 20, 37, 61; IV: 20, 29, 30, 43, 46-54;

V: 3, 5, 6, 25, 51, 59; VI: 1-7, 11, 13, 25, 27, 45-49, 52-55, 57-62, 64-75, 85, 97, 102, 105-110, 121, 122; VIII: 27, 28, 38, 41, 106; IX: 1, 2, 16, 17, 25, 31-36.

k. Classes in which enrolled, including designation as to type of class.

II: 16-18, 32, 41, 44; III: 1, 2, 11, 12, 17, 23, 24, 26-28, 30-34, 37, 38, 41, 42, 44, 45, 46-55, 57-59, 72, 89; IV: 44, 46-48; VI: 1-7, 11, 13, 25, 27, 30, 32-49, 52-55, 57-62, 64-76, 78, 79, 81, 83, 84, 86-88, 105-111, 113, 116-123; VIII: 27, 28, 32; IX: 12-15.

l. Ability group or groups in which enrolled, in general, and for each subject, including extra-curricular groups divided according to ability.

II: 9; III: 17, 72; IV: 43; V: 1-3, 5-11, 13, 15-21, 24-39, 41-43; VI: 1-9, 11, 13-25, 27, 30, 32-49, 52-55, 57-76, 78, 79, 81, 83, 84, 86-88, 105-111, 113, 116-122; VII: 70; VIII: 27, 28, 32, 106; IX: 16, 17, 23, 25-29.

m. Home-room organization of which a member.

VII: 54.

n. Subjects in which enrolled, type of school organization in which subjects are being taken being specified.

II: 9; III: 2, 3, 17, 20; IV: 1-22, 27, 29, 30, 40, 41, 46, 47, 49-57; V: 6, 9, 36-38, 40; VI: 29; VII: 1-13, 15-31, 33-39, 41, 43, 44, 49, 50, 51; VIII: 13, 34, 82, 106; IX: 7, 9, 12-17, 25.

o. Grades earned.

IV: 20; V: 16, 26, 33, 34, 43; VII: 34, 36, 37, 41, 61.

(1) Rank in class or teacher's estimate of ability.

V: 13, 16.

p. Activities in which enrolled, including those which lie outside the regular curriculum, such as extra-curricular activities, sometimes calling for leadership with considerable responsibility attached, valuable home activities, etc.

IV: 27; V: 9; VI: 77; VII: 1-13, 15-31, 33-39, 43, 44, 46, 47, 49-53, 56; VIII: 38, 41, 55-59, 61, 69, 93, 106.

q. Extra-curricular activities in which engaged, including those directed specifically at deficiencies and those calling for qualities of leadership; also extra-curricular activities that lead to or prepare for other extra-curricular activities; also activities having to do with the government of the school.

VII: 54-57, 59, 62, 65-69.

r. Details of past schooling in other school systems. (This indicates the desirability of securing from the school previously attended as complete records as possible.)

IX: 34.

2. Data for the permanent cumulative record that pertain particularly to physical education.

a. Specific physical activities in which engaged, including intramural and inter-school games, physical education program and the teams on which the pupil has participated.
V: 44-47, 49-56; VII: 59, 60, 61; VIII: 109-127.

3. Data for the permanent cumulative record that pertain particularly to vocational matters.

a. Record of guidance and the attempt to find the proper vocation.
IV: 31; VII: 47, 48; IX: 3.

b. Vocation for which being fitted or preparing.
III: 13, 39, 40, 42, 63-66; IV: 20; VII: 46, 47.

4. Data for the permanent cumulative record that pertain particularly to health.

a. Medical aid furnished.
III: 56, 85.

b. Physical defects removed or corrected, including refraction. (Include those removed or corrected by agencies other than school.)
II: 6; III: 23, 24, 26-28, 30-35, 37, 38, 70.

5. Data to be recorded as a part of a day-to-day record, probably in a plan book.[2]

a. Groups within a room in which placed.
V: 12, 18, 23.

b. Extent to which goals are differentiated for each ability level.
VIII: 29.

c. Activities in which engaged, including those that call for outside reading with set of interpretative questions sometimes added; instrumental lessons and freehand drawing; projects organized into large units and demanding a high standard of achievement, reaching into many fields which the child would otherwise miss; extra reading assignments in the content subjects.
VIII: 62-68.

d. Adaptation of curriculum or course of study and method. Other data collected reveal the detail. (This is the general purpose of the plan book.)
II: 43; III: 120; V: 24, 59, 61; VI: 100, 105; VII: 17, 22; VIII: 1, 4, 5, 21, 87.

e. Extent to which permitted to follow special interests, including special interests in reading.
VII: 49-51, 53; VIII: 62-68.

[2] A summary of the day-to-day record probably should appear on the permanent cumulative record.

f. Social adjustments, such as: Specific training given in overcoming undesirable social attitudes and habits; provision for overcoming deficiencies in appearance and in language; steps taken to correct deficiencies in table manners; steps taken to dissipate timidity; steps taken to overcome undesirable personal habits; steps taken to bring about proper attitudes; steps taken to remove spirit of selfishness and unwillingness to give and take.
VII: 45; VIII: 96-102.

g. Specific effort made to develop abilities such as those in music, plastic art, painting, drawing, sketching, building of models, research in science, such as radio, expression and dancing.
VII: 92.

h. Individual adjustments made in the physical education program.
V: 50.

i. Training in leadership given.
V: 49; VII: 64.

j. Extent and nature of drill given.
VIII: 8-16, 18, 19, 43-47, 51, 89.

k. Work missed that is necessary for continuance in school.

B. *To Be Obtained for Those Above Average in Ability.*

1. General data for the permanent cumulative record.
   a. Program of acceleration planned.
   VIII: 42.
   b. Provisional extra credit given for enriched work carried.
   VI: 112.

2. Data to be recorded as part of a day-to-day record.
   a. Stimulation furnished the group through the environment set up.
   VIII: 40.
   b. Enrichment provided, including materials in history and literature, used for enrichment and materials in arithmetic used, such as biographies of mathematicians and history of mathematics.
   VI: 55, 56, 68; VII: 18; VIII: 76, 79.
   c. Adjustments made in subjects calling for a more complete mastery, a broader field of knowledge and a more extensive application of principles.
   VIII: 82.
   d. Extent to which general directions and general questions are used; general principles are discussed; more extensive application of principles made; interference is guarded against in order to give the exploring tendency free play.
   VIII: 71, 73, 75.

    e. Extent to which assignments call for different applications.
      VIII: 72.
    f. Extent to which accuracy and thoroughness are stressed.
      VIII: 50.
    g. Extent to which freedom is allowed in planning.
      V: 62.
    h. Steps taken to develop latent abilities.
      VIII: 70.
    i. Extent of emphasis on academic activities.
      VIII: 81.

C. *To Be Obtained for Those Both Above and Below Average in
Ability.*

  1. Data to be recorded as part of a day-to-day record.
    a. Complexity of material assigned or the complexity of the learning situation.
      VIII: 22, 23, 71.
    b. Time devoted to the mastery of the usual subjects as compared with the time spent by the average pupil on these particular subjects.
      VIII: 36, 37, 39, 54.

D. *To Be Obtained for Those Below Average in Ability.*

  1. Data to be recorded as part of a day-to-day record.
    a. Means of stimulation used to meet individual needs.
      VIII: 24.
    b. Methods of presentation and illustrating used.
      VIII: 23.
    c. Concrete illustrations and continuous specific applications of general principles used.
      VIII: 25.
    d. Training in habitual-responses behavior patterns.
      VIII: 20.
    e. Load carried in subjects in which pupils are apt and in which they are deficient.
      VIII: 33, 34.
    f. Standards of achievement set.
      VIII: 26.

  2. Data for the permanent cumulative record that pertain particularly to vocational matters.
    a. Activity of the school in finding employment.
      VI: 31-33.

E. *To Be Obtained for Those Deficient in the Appreciation of the Æsthetic, in the Understanding of Music and Art, and in the Utilization of Leisure Time.*

I. To be recorded as part of a day-to-day record.

    a. Specific training given in removing defects in appreciation of the æsthetic; in understanding of music and art and in the utilization of leisure time. VIII: 103-105.

F. *To Be Obtained for All Those Who Are Below Standard in Achievement Whether in Corrective Classes or Not.*

I. To be recorded as part of a day-to-day record.

    a. Extent and specific character of coaching assistance given, including all work given for correcting deficiencies and statement as to where the corrective work is being taken. II: 20-30, 33-40; III: 123-126; IV: 48; VI: 15, 19, 26, 38, 39; VII: 40, 41; VIII: 7, 17, 30, 31, 83, 85, 86-91; IX: 1.

G. *To Be Obtained for Mental Subnormals.*

I. General data for the permanent cumulative record.

    a. Record of segregation by sexes. II: 15.

    b. Record of provision for transportation to and from school. II: 12.

    c. Record of exclusion from public school. II: 5.

H. *To Be Obtained for Those Above the Elementary School Level.*

I. General data for the permanent cumulative record.

    a. How classified. IV: 57.

    b. Sequence of subjects set up for the pupil. IX: 11.

    c. Curriculum in which enrolled, changes in the subjects and the course being noted. III: 21; IV: 40, 41; VI: 28, 41, 45, 123; VII: 1-17, 19-31, 33-39; VIII: 32, 106; IX: 7-9, 12-15.

    d. Change in subjects and course. IX: 7, 8.

    e. Credit awarded, including specification of that which does not apply to graduation. IV: 56, 57; VI: 28, 31-49, 52-55, 57-62, 64, 76, 78, 79, 81, 83, 84, 86-88, 105-111, 113, 116-121, 123; VII: 42; VIII: 27, 28.

f. Deficiencies in credits—credits withheld.
  VII: 42.
g. Credit loss suffered by change in courses.
  IX: 10, 14.
h. Restrictions on graduation due to junior high school subjects.
  VI: 113.
i. Restrictions on graduation due to junior high school level of achievement.
  VI: 114.
j. Entrance to college.
  VI: 123.

I. *To Be Obtained for Those in Continuation School.*

  1. General data for the permanent cumulative record.
  a. Type of training received in continuation school.
    IV: 24, 25.

J. *To Be Obtained for Those in Fresh-Air Classes.*

  1. To be recorded as part of a day-to-day record.
  a. Amount of sleep secured in school.
    III: 69.
  b. Kind of food secured at school.
    III: 69.

K. *To Be Obtained for Those Who Are Indentured.*

  1. General data for the permanent cumulative record.
  a. Vocation at which indentured.
    IV: 27.

L. *To Be Obtained for Those Who Are Receiving Special Treatment Because of Physical Deficiencies.*

  1. General data for the permanent cumulative record.
  a. Special classroom facilities provided.
    III: 3, 10, 14, 18, 90, 93, 95-100, 118; VIII: 108.
  b. Time schedule of attendance at special class.
    III: 19.
  c. Corrective work offered.
    III: 2, 3, 10, 12, 14, 17, 23, 24, 26-28, 30-34, 35, 37, 38, 44, 47-55, 57-59, 60, 62-67, 93, 95, 98, 100-117; IV: 39; VIII: 116-120.
  d. Extent to which treatment is individual, including limitations of hours of study, avoidance of competition, removal from school in extreme cases.
    III: 49; VIII: 116-120.

e. Transportation provided to and from school.
III: 10.
f. Home and other out-of-school teaching provided.
III: 4-8, 92.

M. *To Be Obtained for Those Concerning Whom a Clinical Record Is Necessary.*

1. General data for the permanent cumulative record.
    a. Psychopathic and other adjustments made.
    III: 131-138.
    b. Record of clinical investigation.
    III: 129; IX: 8.

N. *To Be Obtained for Those Who Are in Ability Groups.*

1. General data for the permanent cumulative record.
    a. Number in grade within school within which enrolled.
    V: 24.

O. *To Be Obtained for Those in Financial Difficulty.*

1. General data for the permanent cumulative record.
    a. Financial assistance rendered.
    VII: 44.

P. *To Be Obtained for Those Not Particularly Able in Music, Art, or Foreign Language.*

1. General data for the permanent cumulative record.
    a. Steps taken to develop specific interests in music, art, and foreign languages, for instance.
    VIII: 94.

Q. *To Be Obtained for Those Who Have Skipped Units of Work.*

1. General data for the permanent cumulative record.
    a. Extent to which work missed by skipping is made to serve instead of enrichment material.
    VIII: 84.

APPENDIX

The following pages reproduce the assembled material from which the first nine policies of Chapter II were secured. All other policies were taken from a similar compilation of data which is on file in the Library of Teachers College, Columbia University. An explanation of the symbolism following the first statement in the accompanying tabulated material will make clear the procedure to be followed in using these data.

The statement, "There should be special classes for the mentally subnormal," was endorsed in the references indicated by the numerical code. The first of each pair of numbers refers to the reference assigned that number in the Bibliography appearing on page 94 to 97 of this study. The second number of each pair specifies the page of that reference. For instance, 10:365 is to be read: Page 365 of reference 10. The principle relative to provision for the mentally subnormal was wholeheartedly accepted, questioned, or rejected by the cities or individuals indicated by the letter code. A city was represented as reacting in a certain manner when the superintendent, or one acting for him, so reacted, or when the attitude of a number of responsible individuals in the city tended in a certain direction. A certain letter, for instance "A," represents throughout the study the same city or individual unless specific information to the contrary is given. The key to the letter code is on file with the other material in the library of Teachers College, Columbia University. While no negative responses are found in the few pages of the basic data reproduced, there were a number of such responses in connection with certain phases of the work. However, as was previously indicated, a preponderance of affirmative responses was to be expected since the endorsement of at least one reference or of an individual of experience or note was secured before any inquiry was made in the field.

PROVISION FOR THOSE WHO ARE MENTALLY AND SCHOLASTICALLY SUBNORMAL

PROVISION FOR THOSE WHO ARE MENTALLY DEFECTIVE

1. There should be special classes for the mentally subnormal.

> 10: 365; 14: 38, 39; 30: 304; 41: 211; 51: 291, 292; 54: 17; 55: 10; 56: 15; 58: 71; 60: 410, 415; 63: 177; 64: 174.
> Yes: A, B, C, D, E, F, G, I, J, P, R, S.
> B. In a large system, yes. Cannot be used as a panacea. We have, instead, a remedial teacher who retests and sometimes gives remedial instruction. She has considerable administrative power.
> C. Classes for distinct subnormals are called Binet classes. 50 to 75

I. Q. is the usual range. If there is not too great a difference in I. Q., families are put together in Binet classes. Some 70 to 80 I. Q. children are taken if they seem to be very slow. Children as low as 45 I. Q. are taken in where there appears to be some language difficulty. Dull physical defectives are put in these classes also.

E. They are held in various schools. The boys go to pre-vocational school at 13 years, 6 months, but the girls stay in elementary school classes, doing worth-while work, until they are 16 or 17.

H. Considerable criticism of parents feared. The classes have been talked about too much.

K. Have such provision.

L. Situation not ideal here. Twenty-two classes for those who are slow but not feeble-minded. Other pupils are put into the classes, however, for want of a better place, who are social misfits, restoration cases, disciplinary cases, also speech and sight-saving cases. Fortunately, classes are small which enables teachers to do almost individual work.

M. The superintendent thinks it is often possible to care for these pupils in the regular classes if the work is pretty well individualized. There are some classes for subnormals, but they do not include all pupils who might be candidates.

N. Not yet done very thoroughly. Children should not go into these classes until after attendance at school for a year or so because of uncertainty as to the results of tests given kindergarten and first grade children.

R. Rather, there should be five-fold classification.

X. Have a pre-vocational school which takes the children at least two years retarded at about the fourth grade level and gives them general training, training in citizenship, etc., until 15, or as soon thereafter as they wish to withdraw from school.

BASES FOR ADMISSION TO SPECIAL CLASSES

1. Bases for selecting boys and girls for such classes are:

   19: 88; 51: 321, 322; 55: 17, 18, 27; 59: 126.

A. Use I. Q. and physical condition, corroborating with teacher's judgment. I. Q. should be below 75.

B. Probably 60 I. Q. or lower. No classes here, however.

D. About the same as at (E). Retest every year.

E. Roughly, below 80 I. Q. and above 50 or 55 I. Q.

G. Roughly 50 to 70 I. Q. Locate them by the second grade if possible. Give the individual Binet and retest every two years.

I. Same as for (G). Select by nine years of age. There are also classes for border-line cases which are selected by the ninth year.

J. The "A" classes, 66 of them, are for children below 70 I. Q., ages 6 to 13. There are now 19 centers housing these children. The "B" classes are for those who are above 13, whose mental age is below 10 years. Those retarded three or more years are also admitted. The "A" and "B" classes get two or three per cent of all the pupils. I. Q. is determined on the basis of individual tests. Teacher judgment is also used.

N. Basically, an I. Q. of 80 is used. Open to suggestions, however, on additional factors.

P. Are careful to supplement the Binet test with the pictorial and mechanical tests. The family record is secured by the visiting teacher and turned over to the school psychologist. The physical record is also used. The children should spend at least one year in the regular school. This schooling will oftentimes uncover some spark of intelligence, especially from the children of the foreign district. When the child is finally selected perhaps other members of the family can accompany him too, attending regular classes in the school.

R. But such people should really be in the lowest fifth section, thus having one class for each of the elementary grades.

S. Between 70 and 75 I. Q. is the standard used in the state. It is 80 by board ruling in (S). The city gets $200 to $300 a class from the state fund.

2. The feeble-minded and those incapable of ultimate self-maintenance should be educated and cared for by public agencies other than the school system.

> 2: 441; 19: 192; 30: 133; 30: 305; 41: 211.

Yes: B, C, D, G, I, P, R, S, T.

A. Not forced on the parents, but their consent is sought.

C. Children are excluded and are usually put under public care.

J. Two per cent of the two per cent chosen for the special classes enter institutions. They are taken at 45 I. Q. Because of possible parental objection, they may stay at home.

3. Removal of a physical handicap may make a child practically normal. Such a procedure should be tried before placing the child in a special class.

> 51: 70.

Yes: A, T.

A. A physical examination precedes the individual mental examination.

R. A prominent authority was quoted as stating that, after all, 90 per cent of the mental deficiency is real.

Wallin makes this comment regarding the relation of physical condition to teachableness:

> Medical or physical treatment is the first measure of relief to give defective children. It will prove to be a valuable aid in many cases, but it should be regarded as an aid and not as a panacea for mental inefficiency. It will not remedy all mental and educational disabilities. Its influence will sometimes be wholly negative. Moreover, often when the physical treatment proves efficacious it must be followed by a special educational regime. But since the results of the medical treatment frequently cannot be foreseen, it should be

included as an experimental preliminary step in our program of educational reconstruction for the mentally handicapped.[1]

PROCEDURE WHEN A SPECIAL CLASS IS NOT POSSIBLE

1. If a special class cannot be organized, work must be adjusted within the class to those who are below normal in ability.

   58: 76.

   Yes: A, B, C, D, E, F, M, R, S, T.

   E. Special classes cover the situation pretty well here.
   F. But segregation eases the load tremendously.
   M. This method has great possibilities.

GRADING SPECIAL CLASS PUPILS

1. In the larger centers, classes for the mental subnormals should be divided according to age and mentality.

   52: 50, 51.

   Yes: C, I, R. T.

   A. Chronological age is satisfactory.
   D. Grade according to achievement if the number is sufficient.
   E. Educational age is also used.
   G. They are divided in the centers according to mental age. If the division is carried out before they come to the moron centers, it is on the same basis.
   L. Mental age and educational age are used.
   N. The sectioning is not yet done very carefully.

[1] J. E. Wallace Wallin, *The Education of the Mentally Handicapped,* p. 108.

BIBLIOGRAPHY [1]

Books and Bulletins

1. BAKER, HARRY J. *Characteristic Differences in Bright and Dull Pupils.* Public School Publishing Co., 1927.
2. BAKER, SARA JOSEPHINE. *Child Hygiene.* Harper and Bros., 1925.
3. BRACE, DAVID K. *Measuring Motor Ability.* A. S. Barnes & Co., 1927.
4. BRIGGS, H. L. *The Cleveland Plan for Apprentice Training.* Board of Education, Cleveland, Ohio, 1926.
5. BRIGGS, THOMAS H. *The Junior High School.* Classroom Teacher, Inc., 1927.
6. BRUNER, HERBERT B. *The Junior High School at Work.* Bureau of Publications, Teachers College, Columbia University, 1925.
7. BUCKINGHAM, BURDETTE ROSS. *Research for Teachers.* Silver, Burdett and Co., 1926.
8. BUCKNER, CHESTER A. *Educational Diagnosis of Individual Pupils.* Bureau of Publications, Teachers College, Columbia University, 1919.
9. COY, GENEVIEVE LENORE. *The Interests, Abilities and Achievements of a Special Class for Gifted Children.* Bureau of Publications, Teachers College, Columbia University, 1923.
10. CUBBERLEY, E. P. *The Principal and His School.* Houghton Mifflin Co., 1923.
11. CUNNINGHAM, BESS V. *The Prognostic Value of a Primary Group Test.* Bureau of Publications, Teachers College, Columbia University, 1923.
12. DAVIS, MARY DABNEY. *General Practice in Kindergarten Education in the United States.* National Education Association, 1925.
13. DICKSON, VIRGIL E. *The Use of Mental Tests in School Administration.* Board of Education, Berkeley, California, 1922.
14. DICKSON, VIRGIL E. AND TERMAN, LEWIS. *Provisions for Individual Differences in Junior High School.* Classroom Teacher, Inc., 1927.
15. EDGERTON, ALANSON H. *Vocational Guidance and Counseling.* The Macmillan Co., 1926.
16. FREEMAN, FRANK N. AND DOUGHERTY, MARY L. *How to Teach Handwriting.* Houghton Mifflin Co., 1923.
17. HOLLINGSHEAD, ARTHUR DACK. *An Evaluation of the Use of Certain Educational and Mental Measurements for Purposes of Classification.* Bureau of Publications, Teachers College, Columbia University, 1928.

[1] The complete bibliography, consisting of two hundred seventy-nine titles, from which the suggested policies were originally taken, is on file in the Teachers College Library, as a part of the unpublished appendix. Only the most significant and readily obtainable references are given here.

18. HOLLINGWORTH, LETA S. *Gifted Children. Their Nature and Nurture.* The Macmillan Co., 1926.

19. HORN, JOHN LOUIS. *The Education of Exceptional Children.* The Century Co., 1924.

20. IRWIN, ELIZABETH A. AND MARKS, L. A. *Fitting the School to the Child.* The Macmillan Co., 1924.

21. JOINT COMMITTEE ON HEALTH PROBLEMS IN EDUCATION OF THE NATIONAL EDUCATION ASSOCIATION and the American Medical Association, with the Coöperation of the National Society for the Prevention of Blindness. *Conserving the Sight of School Children.* National Education Association, 1201 Sixteenth St., Washington, D.C.

22. JOINT COMMITTEE ON HEALTH PROBLEMS IN EDUCATION OF THE NATIONAL EDUCATION ASSOCIATION, and the American Medical Association, with the Coöperation of the American Federation for the Hard of Hearing and the New York League for the Hard of Hearing, Inc. *The Deafened School Child.* National Education Association, 1201 Sixteenth St., Washington, D.C.

23. KELLER, FRANKLIN J. *Day Schools for Young Workers.* The Century Co., 1924.

24. KELLEY, TRUMAN LEE. *Interpretation of Educational Measurements.* World Book Co., 1927.

25. KITSON, HARRY DEXTER. *The Psychology of Vocational Adjustment.* J. B. Lippincott Co., 1925.

26. KOOS, LEONARD V. *The American Secondary School.* Ginn and Co., 1927.

27. McCALL, WILLIAM A. *How to Measure in Education.* The Macmillan Co., 1922.

28. McKOWN, HARRY C. *Extra-Curricular Activities.* The Macmillan Co., 1927.

29. MARVIN, CLOYD HECK. *Commercial Education in Secondary Schools.* Henry Holt & Co., 1922.

30. MORT, PAUL R. *The Individual Pupil in the Management of Class and School.* American Book Co., 1928.

31. MYERS, GEORGE E. *The Problem of Vocational Guidance.* The Macmillan Co., 1927.

32. PECK, ANNETTA W., SAMUELSON, ESTELLE E., and LEHMAN, ANN. *Ears and the Man.* F. A. Davis Co., 1926.

33. PROCTOR, WILLIAM MARTIN. *The Use of Psychological Tests in the Educational and Vocational Guidance of High School Pupils.* Public School Publishing Co., 1923.

34. REAVIS, W. C. *Guidance in the Junior High School.* Classroom Teacher, Inc., 1927.

35. REAVIS, W. C. *Pupil Adjustment in Junior and Senior High School.* D. C. Heath and Co., 1926.

36. REED, MARY M. *An Investigation of Practices in First Grade Admission and Promotion.* Bureau of Publications, Teachers College, Columbia University, 1927.

37. ROGERS, FREDERICK RAND. *Test and Measurement Programs in the*

Redirection of Physical Education. Bureau of Publications, Teachers College, Columbia University, 1927.

38. Ross, Clay Campbell. *The Relation Between Grade School Record and High School Achievement.* Bureau of Publications, Teachers College, Columbia University, 1925.

39. Ryan, H. H. and Crecelius, Philipine. *Ability Grouping in the Junior High School.* Harcourt, Brace and Co., Inc., 1927.

40. Rynearson, Edward, Chairman. *Guidance in Secondary Schools.* National Association of Secondary School Principals, 1928.

41. Sears, Jesse B. *The School Survey.* Houghton Mifflin Co., 1925.

42. Seashore, Carl E. *The Psychology of Musical Talent.* Silver, Burdett and Co., 1919.

43. Stevenson, P. R. *Smaller Classes or Larger.* Public School Publishing Co., 1923.

44. Stowell, Agnes, Samuelson, Estelle E., and Lehman, Ann. *Lip Reading for the Deafened Child.* The Macmillan Co., 1928.

45. Symonds, Percival M. *Measurement in Secondary Education.* The Macmillan Co., 1927.

46. Terman, L. M. *The Intelligence of School Children.* Houghton Mifflin Co., 1919.

47. Thayer, V. T. *The Passing of the Recitation.* D. C. Heath and Co., 1928.

48. Toops, Herbert A. *Tests for Vocational Guidance of Children Thirteen to Sixteen.* Bureau of Publications, Teachers College, Columbia University, 1923.

49. Wallin, J. E. Wallace. *The Education of Handicapped Children.* Houghton Mifflin Co., 1924.

50. Wentworth, Mary M. *Individual Differences in the Intelligence of School Children.* Harvard University Press, 1926.

51. Wood, Thomas D. and Rowell, Hugh G. *Health Supervision and Medical Inspection of Schools.* W. B. Saunders Co., 1927.

Superintendents' Reports

52. Detroit. *Eighty-third Annual Report of the Detroit Public Schools.* Board of Education, 1926.

53. Mount Vernon, New York. "The Individual Child in the Schools," *Annual Report.* Board of Education, 1922.

54. Philadelphia. *Annual Report of the Superintendent of Public Schools.* Board of Education, 1925.

School Surveys

55. Alexandria, Virginia, Survey. Government Printing Office, 1924.

56. The Cape Towns on Cape Cod Survey. *Education in Twelve Cape Towns.* Ambrose Press, 1927.

57. Jamestown Eye Survey. University of State of New York Press, 1926.

58. Mort, Paul R. *An Educational Program for Haworth, New Jersey.* (Manuscript), Teachers College, Columbia University, 1927.

59. MISSISSIPPI SURVEY. *A State Educational System at Work.* Bernard B. Jones Fund, 1927.

60. RACINE, WISCONSIN. *The Racine School Survey.* Board of Education, 1926.

61. SEASHORE, CARL E. *A Survey of Musical Talent in the Public Schools.* First Series, No. 37, University of Iowa, November, 1920.

62. STRAYER, GEORGE D., ENGELHARDT, N. L., AND OTHERS. *Survey of the Schools of Duval County, Florida, Including Jacksonville.* School Survey Series, Bureau of Publications, Teachers College, Columbia University, 1927.

63. STRAYER, GEORGE D., ENGELHARDT, N. L., AND OTHERS. *Report of the Survey of the Schools of Lynn, Massachusetts.* School Survey Series, Bureau of Publications, Teachers College, Columbia University, 1927.

64. STRAYER, GEORGE D., ENGELHARDT, N. L., AND OTHERS. *Report of the Survey of the Schools of Port Arthur, Texas.* Bureau of Publications, Teachers College, Columbia University, 1926.

YEARBOOKS

65. DEPARTMENT OF SUPERINTENDENCE. *Fifth Yearbook,* 1927; *Sixth Yearbook,* 1928. National Education Association.

66. NATIONAL SOCIETY FOR THE STUDY OF EDUCATION. *Twenty-third Yearbook, Part I,* 1924; *Twenty-fourth Yearbook, Part II,* 1925; *Twenty-fifth Yearbook, Part II,* 1926; *Twenty-sixth Yearbook, Part II,* 1927; *Twenty-seventh Yearbook, Part II,* 1928. Public School Publishing Co.

67. NORTH CENTRAL ASSOCIATION. *Twenty-third Annual Meeting of the North Central Association of Colleges and Secondary Schools.* North Central Association, 1928.